The Iron Flute

The Iron Flute

100 *Zen Kōan*
with commentary by Genrō, Fūgai, and Nyogen
Translated and edited by
Nyogen Senzaki and Ruth Strout McCandless
Illustrated by Toriichi Murashima
CHARLES E. TUTTLE COMPANY
Rutland, Vermont & Tokyo, Japan

Representatives

For Continental Europe:
BOXERBOOKS, INC., *Zurich*

For the British Isles:
PRENTICE-HALL INTERNATIONAL, INC., *London*

For Australasia:
BOOK WISE (AUSTRALIA) PTY. LTD.
1 Jeanes Street, Beverley 5009, South Australia

Published by the Charles E. Tuttle Company, Inc.
of Rutland, Vermont & Tokyo, Japan
with editorial offices at Suido 1-chome, 2-6, Bunkyo-ku, Tokyo

Copyright in Japan, 1964, by Charles E. Tuttle Company, Inc.

Library of Congress Catalog Card No. 60-11512
International Standard Book No. 0-8048-0266-1

First edition, 1964
Second printing, 1985

PRINTED IN JAPAN

Table of Contents

List of Illustrations

Foreword

THE TRANSLATION of *Tetteki Tōsui,* or *The Iron Flute,* was begun in June 1939 by Nyogen Senzaki, who used the stories with their commentaries as lectures for his own students. He preferred to dictate the story and commentary to a student, who would then loan the manuscript to other students to copy for their own use. When I met Mr. Senzaki, I began to collect and compile the scattered manuscripts, and soon after was at work with him on new translations.

Nyogen Senzaki left California in 1942, but continued to send me translations and comments to "polish." On his return in 1945, his students gathered around him, and he read his lectures. Toward the end of this series, he considered his students well acquainted with Zen ways, and altered the style of his translations. He now supplied very little comment of his own, but used Genrō's and Fūgai's more freely. An occasional comment by one of Nyogen's own group also appears in the later kōan.

Zen is a path of discipline and development unique in religion or philosophy. A person unfamiliar with its tenets may find the dialogues recorded here obscure, if not downright confusing. It may even seem that every step of the way is deliberately blocked by the teacher in an effort to conceal rather than reveal the teachings—often even at the cost of physical pain on the part of the disciple. Since it is impossible here to go into the history of Zen, or to clarify its aims or methods, a bibliography has been added for the interested reader who wishes more background.

The illustrations have all been obtained through the kind efforts of Sōen Nakagawa, head of Ryūtaku-ji, famous Zen temple in Mishima, Shizuoka Prefecture.

The end papers reproduce a section from a hanging scroll depicting the "Five Hundred Arhats" by Fūgai, chief disciple of Genrō and annotator of the original *Tetteki Tōsui*, who also did the portrait of Genrō shown on page 16. The "Five Hundred Arhats" is reproduced by the kind permission of its present owner, Mr. Seizō Suzuki of Hamamatsu; and the Genrō portrait by permission of Ryūman-ji, Hyōgo Prefecture.

The masterful ink paintings which illustrate the text, commissioned by the publishers especially for this volume, were painted by Mr. Toriichi Murashima as a tribute to the late Senzaki-san after several months of meditation upon the *Tetteki Tōsui*. Mr. Murashima is a distinguished representative of contemporary Japanese painting in the traditional manner and is particularly noted for the Zen outlook that permeates his work and for his lifelong study of the depiction of rocks in both their objective and metaphysical aspects.

Except for the more commonly known Japanese names of Buddhist sects, Chinese and Japanese proper names, respectively, have been given in their original readings. Since, however, a number af Zen works in English have used Japanese readings for Chinese names, an appendix has been added for the convenience of the interested reader giving both the Japanese and Chinese names with the original characters. Japanese names are rendered Western style, surname last.

RUTH STROUT MCCANDLESS

Introduction

THE ORIGINAL of the present work was written and published in 1783 by Genrō, a Zen master of the Sōtō school in Japan. Each story is a kōan on which the author makes his comment and writes a poem. Fūgai, Genrō's successor, added his remarks, sentence by sentence, to his teacher's book. I will translate the stories or main subjects, including in most cases Genrō's comments and Fūgai's remarks as reference. Occasionally a poem will be translated to encourage study. Since many of Genrō's and Fūgai's comments refer to old stories and customs unknown in the Occident, I shall explain them in my commentary.

With the exception of a few stories from India, the background is China during the T'ang (A.D. 620–906) and Sung (930–1278) dynasties, the Golden Age of Zen.

Tetteki Tōsui is the name of the original text. *Tetteki* means "iron flute." Usually a flute is made of bamboo with a mouthpiece and several sideholes for the fingers, but this flute is a solid iron rod with neither mouthpiece nor finger holes. *Tōsui* means "to blow it upside down." The ordinary musician who wanders among the lines of the grand staff will never be able to handle this Zen instrument, but one who plays the stringless harp can also play this flute with no mouthpiece.

> *The moon floats above the pines,*
> *And the night veranda is cold*
> *As the ancient, clear sound comes from your finger tips.*

The old melody usually makes the listeners weep,
But Zen music is beyond sentiment.
Do not play again unless the Great Sound of Lao-tsu
accompanies you.

HSÜEH-TOU (980–1052)
Chinese Zen Master

Lao-tsu said, "Great utensils take a long time to make. Great characters never were built in a few years. Great sound is the sound which transcends ordinary sound."

Now you know why the book was named *Tetteki Tōsui,* or "Blowing Upside Down the Solid Iron Flute." It is a book of the "sound of one hand." It is the daily life of Zen.

NYOGEN SENZAKI

The Iron Flute

Genrō by Fūgai: Portrait of the master by his chief disciple, still in the possession of Ryūman-ji, the temple where Genrō compiled the original Tetteki Tōsui.

1. Manjusri Enters the Gate

One day Manjusri stood outside the gate when Buddha called to him. "Manjusri, Manjusri, why do you not enter?"

"I do not see a thing outside the gate. Why should I enter?" Manjusri answered.

NYOGEN: Zen stories are the problems of life, the themes of meditation. It is not necessary that the dialogue be made by Buddha and Manjusri. Suppose one of you hesitated to enter this Zen-dō, and I said, "Why don't you come in?" If he is awakened at that moment, he may say, "I do not see anything outside this Zen-dō. Why should I come in?" He sees nothing separated from the Zen-dō; "in" and "out" are terms of comparison. Essentially he hears nothing, sees nothing, touches nothing, smells nothing, tastes nothing, and thinks nothing, but takes his place gracefully and seats himself. What else can I do but praise such a person of perfect freedom?

Man is still young and stupid. He learns duality instead of unity from religions. With his illusion man occasionally builds the gate, then sees something outside it. He hears, smells, tastes, touches, and thinks from his egoistic standpoint. He talks of universal brotherhood, but does not realize the principle of it. The world needs Manjusri, not a messiah or a prophet. Who is Manjusri?

Manjusri symbolizes Buddha's wisdom. He rides a lion, crushing all delusions, and with his sharp sword cuts all entanglements that prevent emancipation. Some Buddhists think Manjusri was a disciple of Buddha Sakyamuni; others talk about his past life and present existence miraculously revealed. Let them dream as they wish. Zen students must meet Manjusri within themselves.

The Avatamçaka Sutra mentions four worlds: the world of matter, the world of reason, the world of harmony in reason and matter, and the world of harmonious materials. The Manjusri of our story lives beyond the world of matter in the world of reason, but he has not yet learned to harmonize the two.

Samantabhadra symbolizes Buddha's loving-kindness. He rides an elephant, patiently driving it through the jungles, loving and respecting all sentient beings. He will not declare a reason as Manjusri did, but will quietly pass the gate. His heart is Buddha's heart, answering the call of Buddha like an echo.

The fourth world of the Avatamçaka Sutra is sometimes referred to as the "Kingdom of Heaven." To enter this stage, mankind must learn to live in the world of harmony in reason and matter, and before this he must live in the world of reason. It is very important to meet Manjusri face to face in our day. He says, "I do not see a thing outside the gate. Why should I enter?" Now, where is the gate? Are you yourself inside or outside the gate?

2. Opening Speech of Lo-shan

Lord Min-wang built a monastery for Lo-shan and asked him to make the first speech in the lecture hall. As master of the institution, Lo-shan sat on a chair, but spoke no word except, "Farewell," before returning to his own room. Lord Min-wang approached him saying, "Even Buddha's teaching at Gradharkuta Mountain must have been the same as yours of today." Lo-shan answered, "I thought you were a stranger to the teaching, but now I discover you know something of Zen."

NYOGEN: These two men lived in China in the eighth century A.D., but they will always show the beauty of incompleteness to those who understand inner appreciation. A Buddhist chapel usually has a statue of Buddha above the altar, but a true Zen temple has no image. A master takes the place of Buddha, using the altar as a pulpit; he brings the robe he has inherited genealogically, putting it on before his lecture and taking it off immediately after. Our Lo-shan must have done the same thing. The original Chinese says, "He took his seat, put on his robe, took it off and said, 'Farewell.' His discourse, thus, was ended." Good act! But do not let your innocent monks imitate you! It will be worse than having a statue of Buddha. Iconoclasm, which starts as a reaction, is bound to keep itself in an ivory tower. To crush that ivory tower is the real iconoclasm. If Lord Min-wang had been more advanced in Zen, he would have expressed his disappointment in missing the master's discourse even though he understood exactly the silent message of Lo-shan.

The growth of a monastery is as slow and invisible as that of the shrubs and trees surrounding it. The master, monks, and donor have just planted the seeds and can never see their complete fulfillment. Why do they not just enjoy devoting the present day to meditation? This was the teaching Lo-shan inherited from Buddha through generations of disciples.

When I first moved into this humble house, there was no picture of Buddha in the Zen-dō nor any furniture in the house except a piano stool. I sat on this stool silently, folding my hands palm to palm. It was my first lecture in this Zen-dō, and all others since have been nothing but explanations. If some of you plan to give lectures or to write essays on Zen, remind yourselves of this story and say "Farewell" to yourselves happily.

3. Nan-ch'üan's Stone Buddha

Upasaka Liu-kêng said to Nan-ch'üan, "In my house there is a stone which sits up or lies down. I intend to carve it as a Buddha. Can I do it?" Nan-ch'üan answered, "Yes, you can." Upasaka Liu-kêng asked again, "Can I not do it?" Nan-ch'üan answered, "No, you cannot do it."

NYOGEN: This layman wished to know his possibility of becoming Buddha. If he is not able to become Buddha, then he is like a stone. He had thought his teacher, Nan-ch'üan, would praise his good intentions, but all he said was, "Yes, you can." When Liu-kêng said, "Can I not do it?" he wished to make it certain and had expected Nan-ch'üan to give him every assurance.

Nan-ch'üan's Zen uses idealism as its entrance. One who wishes to carve a stone in Buddha's image must do it by himself, whether others approve or not. If he has the slightest doubt of the possibility, he will never do it. What he is now is the result of what he has thought, and what he thinks now forms what he will be in the future. Neither master nor no-master can interfere with this law of causation. Liu-kêng had a good stone, but his determination was not steadfast until he was brushed aside by Nan-ch'üan. It is like the old story of the larks and the farmer. They were not alarmed when they heard the farmer was going to cut his wheat with his neighbor's help, but when they learned the farmer had decided to cut it by himself without help, they left the nest and flew away. Liu-kêng later became a very good student.

GENRŌ: I see one stone which the layman carried to the monastery. I also see another stone which Nan-ch'üan kept in his meditation hall. All the hammers in China cannot crush these two stones.

"Liu-kêng said to Nan-ch'üan, 'In my house there is a stone which sits up or lies down. Can I carve it as a Buddha?'" —From Kōan 3, page 20

4. Pai-ling's Attainment

Pai-ling and Upasaka P'ang-yün were studying under Ma-tsu, the successor of Nan-yüeh. One day as they met on the road, Pai-ling remarked, "Our grandfather of Zen said, 'If one asserts that it is something, one misses it altogether.' I wonder if he ever showed it to anyone." Upasaka P'ang-yün answered, "Yes, he did." "To whom?" asked the monk. The layman then pointed his finger to himself and said, "To this fellow."

"Your attainment," said Pai-ling, "is so beautiful and so profound even Manjusri and Subhuti cannot praise you adequately."

Then the layman said to the monk, "I wonder if there is anyone who knows what our grandfather in Zen meant." The monk did not reply, but put on his straw hat and walked away. "Watch your step," Upasaka P'ang-yün called to him, but Pai-ling walked on without turning his head.

NYOGEN: Zen students strive to realize Buddha-nature. They may name it "mind essence," Dharmakaya, Buddhakaya, or "one's own true self," but names are mere shadows, not the real thing. As Nan-yüeh says, "Even when one asserts that it is something, one misses it altogether."

There is no doubt that both the monk and the layman had attained Nan-yüeh's Zen. The latter, however, still held a trace of attainment, whereas the monk was completely free.

Rennyo, a Hongan-ji abbot, asked Ikkyū, a contemporary master of Zen, "I have heard that you are an enlightened person. Is it true?" "I never did such mischief," Ikkyū answered. It was probably useless to show the abbot such brilliancy of Zen, but it illustrates Pai-ling's action in the story. An Oriental proverb says, "It is useless to show the gold piece to a cat." Zen stories should not be told to outsiders. The layman in this story showed his Zen to a fellow student, but he would not do this in the course of everyday life.

Professor Gronbech of the University of Copenhagen states: "The mystics express essentially the same thoughts at all times; in fact, so much agreement exists between them that they often use the same words and illustrations. One can find almost identical passages from the Indian living thousands of years before our chronology and from the European monk of the later middle ages; even now the modern poet creates utterances which lead thought straight back to the old writings. The reason for their agreement is that they have an experience in common, which is in itself as clear and precise as the observations made by the everyday man in the material world. There is no room here for dreams and fantasies. The mystic is occupied with the experience governing his whole life."

A kōan is a strange thing. As you work on it, it will lead you into the world of experience. The more experience, the clearer your glimpse of Buddha-nature. When you are given a kōan, you can then answer it as naturally as you would your own name.

GENRŌ:
A cloud rests at the mouth of the cave
Doing nothing all day.
The moonlight penetrates the waves throughout the night,
But leaves no trace in the water.

5. Shao-shan's Phrase

A monk once asked Shao-shan, "Is there any phrase which is neither right nor wrong?" Shao-shan answered, "A piece of white cloud does not show any ugliness."

NYOGEN: Shao-shan was successor to Chia-shan, whose severity was well known among the monasteries, but when he had passed through Chia-shan's severity, he was able to convey profound teaching with a word or short sentence.

The monk was really asking, "What is true freedom or

emancipation?" Most of us struggle in the entanglement of right and wrong, good and bad, liking and disliking, but Zen transcends these dualistic thoughts. The moment, however, one speaks of his Zen, a couple of monsters flare in front of him. Shao-shan did not mention absoluteness or oneness, nor any other term of religious jargon. He left these to the people who have made a profession of religion.

GENRŌ:

Not right, not wrong.
I gave you a phrase;
Keep it for thirty years,
But show it to no one.

6. T'ou-tzu's Dinner

A certain Buddhist family in the capital invited T'ou-tzu to dinner. The head of the family set a tray full of grass in front of the monk. T'ou-tzu put his fists on his forehead and raised his thumbs like horns. He was then brought the regular dinner. Later a monk asked T'ou-tzu to explain the reason of his strange action. "Avalokiteçvara Bodhisattva," answered T'ou-tzu.

NYOGEN: No one knows why the head of the family served the grass to T'ou-tzu, but it might have been because it was sometimes believed in ancient China that a monk without realization would be reincarnated as an ox. Today many monks in the Orient sleep and eat like oxen but do not work as hard. T'ou-tzu blamed himself for his disciples, so apologized to the world with his pose of an ox. Zen monks are humorous and usually lighthearted, taking jokes and sarcasm with good will. By the time T'ou-tzu was enjoying the regular meal, he had forgotten the incident of the grass.

The monk, who asked T'ou-tzu about his strange action, was a collector of anecdotes. If I were T'ou-tzu I would not have replied to the monk, but T'ou-tzu was very kindhearted. "Avalokiteçvara Bodhisattva," he answered.

In the Saddharma-pundarika Sutra Avalokiteçvara is said to preach in many shapes. Some Buddhists are afraid of reincarnation, thinking only of themselves and wishing to escape it, but the Bodhisattvas of Mahayana teaching make themselves hundreds and thousands of manifestations for other beings' happiness every day of the week.

7. Yün-mên's Feast in the Joss House

One day as Yün-mên gave a lecture to his monks, he asked them, "Do you want to be acquainted with the old patriarchs?" Before anyone could answer, he pointed his cane above the monks, saying, "The old patriarchs are jumping on your heads." Then he asked, "Do you wish to see the eyes of the old patriarchs?" He pointed to the ground beneath the monks' feet and answered himself, "They are all under your feet." After a moment's pause he spoke as though to himself, "I made a feast in the joss house, but the hungry gods are never satisfied."

NYOGEN: What a masterpiece of the world's short prose! Yünmên's question is as applicable to those of Europe and America today as it was centuries ago in China. Any faker who mentions the reincarnations of masters becomes so popular he makes a fortune. Thousands of people in this country alone are being cheated every day by charlatans, who encourage the most unreasonable and fantastic products of the imagination. But this would not be possible if it were not that some people, who believe in a religion or study a philosophy, are unsatisfied with the true feast. They are like the Chinese idols of a joss house; the fragrance of enlightenment floats around them but they have no sense of smell. Books in libraries, scriptures in temples, hundreds and thousands of them, are offering the true feast in vain to flesh-and-blood idols! Yün-mên wasted the words of his great sermon after all.

GENRŌ: We have only the blue sky above our heads. Where are the old patriarchs? We have only the good earth beneath our feet. Where are the eyes of the old patriarchs? Yün-mên's feast was a mere shadow, no wonder the gods could not appease their hunger. Do you want to know how I make a feast in the joss house? I shut the door and lie down on the floor, stretch my arms and legs and take a nap. Why? Because there is a saying, "A cup brimful cannot hold any more tea. The good earth never produced a hungry man."

8. Yün-chü's Instruction

Yün-chü, a Sōtō master of Chinese Zen, had many disciples. One monk, who came from Korea, said to him, "I have realized something within me which I cannot describe at all." "Why is that so?" asked Yün-chü, "it cannot be difficult." "Then you must do it for me," the monk replied. Yün-chü said, "Korea! Korea!" and closed the dialogue. Later a teacher of the Ōryū school of Zen criticized the incident, "Yün-chü could not understand the monk at all. There was a great sea between them, even though they lived in the same monastery."

NYOGEN: Yün-chü lived in the southeastern part of China in the latter years of the ninth century A.D. The Korean monk came to him from across the Yellow Sea and probably the East China Sea also. His enthusiasm was far above that of most wandering monks. I can picture him meditating day and night until at last he entered Samadhi and discovered his true self as though awaking from a dream. No words of mankind can describe what he attained.

Sōen Shaku once said, "Meditation is not a difficult task. It is a way to lead you to your long-lost home." Yün-chü had had his own experience, so he stated there was no dfficulty in expressing what one has attained. The monk was still in the first flush of his realization, so he requested his teacher to say it for him. The teacher said, "Korea! Korea!" congratulating him on his return home. I appreciate the brotherly love of the teacher, but I must say he did not describe what the monk wanted. He should have waited a few moments and allowed the monk to say it himself. Even so, an exclamation is not a description of attainment. As Master Nan-yüeh said, "Even when one asserts that it is something, one misses it altogether." The monk had asked for something absolutely impossible.

GENRŌ: The Ōryū monk could not understand Yün-chü. There was a great mountain between them even though they were contemporaries.

It is not difficult to open the mouth;
It is not difficult to describe the thing.
The monk from Korea was a wandering mendicant,
Who had not returned home as yet.

9. Tz'u-ming's Summary

Ts'ui-yen, thinking he had attained something of Zen, left T'zu-ming's monastery when he was still a young monk to travel all over China. Years later, when he returned to visit the monastery, his old teacher asked, "Tell me the summary of Buddhism." Ts'ui-yen answered, "If a cloud does not hang over the mountain, the moonlight will penetrate the waves of the lake." T'zu-ming looked at his former pupil in anger, "You are getting old. Your hair has turned white, and your teeth are sparse, yet you still have such an idea of Zen. How can you escape birth and death?" Tears washed Ts'ui-yen's face as he bent his head. After a few minutes he asked, "Please tell me the summary of Buddhism." "If a cloud does not hang over the mountain," the teacher replied, "the moonlight will penetrate the waves of the lake." Before the teacher had finished speaking, Ts'ui-yen was enlightened.

NYOGEN: Without stopping to think that perhaps reality was beyond his imagination, Ts'ui-yen had fooled himself for years with false conceptions. As he traveled, he no doubt spoke freely about Buddhism, borrowing his words from others, and finally he tried to pass the counterfeit on to his teacher. The words themselves were all right as far as they went, but they were not echoed from the bottom of his heart. When T'zu-ming scolded him in anger, Ts'ui-yen's heart was for the first time turned inside out, and he saw his own ugliness. In shame he bent his head, then asked his teacher for the summary of Buddhism. "If a cloud does not hang over the mountain, the moonlight will penetrate the waves of the lake," came the answer. It was not a mere description of a beautiful scene, it was the true message of Buddha-Dharma. If the listener does not realize the truth at such a moment, Zen is a useless thing in the world.

GENRŌ: Ts'ui-yen knew how to steer his boat with the current, but he never dreamed of the stormy course requiring him to go against the stream.

The bellows blew high the flaming forge;
The sword was hammered on the anvil.
It was the same steel as in the beginning,
But how different was its edge!

10. Yüeh-shan Holds It

The governor of a state asked Yüeh-shan, "I understand that all Buddhists must possess Sila (precepts), Dhyana (meditation) and Prajna (wisdom). Do you keep the precepts? Do you practice meditation? Have you attained wisdom?" "This poor monk has no such junk around here," Yüeh-shan replied. "You must have a profound teaching," the governor said, "but I do not understand it." "If you want to hold it," Yüeh-shan continued, "you must climb the highest mountain and sit on the summit or dive into the deepest sea and walk on the bottom. Since you cannot enter even your own bed without a burden on your mind, how can you grasp and hold my Zen?"

NYOGEN: When one keeps the precepts, he can meditate well; when his meditation becomes matured, he attains wisdom. Since these three, Sila, Dhyana, and Prajna, are interrelated and equally essential, no one of the three can be carried as an independent study. But the governor was trying to understand the teaching as he might a civil-service examination. He himself had often selected men who might be deficient in one quality, provided that they were strong in another. What foolish questions to ask Yüeh-shan! If a monk is deficient in the precepts, he cannot accomplish his meditation; if his meditation is not complete, he never attains true wisdom. He cannot specialize in any one of the three.

Today there are Buddhist students who write books but never practice meditation or lead an ethical life and Zen "masters" who lack many of the simpler virtues. Even though they shave their heads, wear yellow robes, and recite the sutras, they never know the true meaning of Dharma. What can you do with these imitators?

The governor could not understand Yüeh-shan's steep Zen, but when he admitted it, Yüeh-shan saw there was hope and proceeded to give him some instruction.

GENRŌ: Yüeh-shan uses the mountain and the sea as an illustration. If you cling to summit or bottom, you will create delusion. How can he hold "it" on the summit or the bottom? The highest summit must not have a top to sit on, and the greatest depth no place to set foot. Even this statement is not expressing the truth. What do you do then? (He turns to the monks.) Go out and work in the garden or chop wood.

FŪGAI: Stop! Stop! Don't try to pull an unwilling cat over the carpet. She will scratch and make the matter worse.

NYOGEN: Now! How are you going to express it?

11. Chao-chou Covers His Head

A monk entered Chao-chou's room to do sanzen, and found him sitting with his head covered by his robe. The monk retreated. "Brother," said Chao-chu, "do not say I did not receive your sanzen."

NYOGEN: Sanzen is unification with Zen. You become Zen and Zen becomes you. In the Rinzai school, when a student enters the teacher's room to receive personal guidance, it is called sanzen to distinguish it from zazen, which is medita-

會麼別畫不如花有笑
離情難似竹無心

"T'ou-tzu's efforts to save all sentient beings are
no better than the blossoming flowers of spring."
—From a comment by Genrō on Kōan 6

tion alone or with others. In the Sōtō school it is said that sanzen is zazen, so they devote themselves to meditation but seldom give or receive guidance.

This place belongs neither to Rinzai nor Sōtō, and this monk never claimed to be a teacher. When you come and meditate sincerely, I will join you in the Zen-dō. When you ask a question on Zen, I will answer with my Zen. The most important thing is for you to become Zen and Zen to become you. I am nobody from the beginning, but I may encourage your meditation or solve your doubts. Do not hasten to work one kōan after another as you might solve algebra problems, nor keep on a drowsy meditation without stimulation of personal guidance.

It was probably a cold evening, and Chao-chou covered his head with his robe, heavy with mending and stitching. Since the monk had no right to enter his teacher's room for anything but Zen, why did he hesitate and retreat? Fūgai said, "The monk was a stupid fellow, thinking the master slept like any other absent-minded person. But even a sleeping tiger has a strong vibration around it. The monk was like a person passing through a diamond mine with empty hands." See the brilliancy of Chao-chou's loving-kindness when he says, "Brother, do not say I did not receive your sanzen." The monk should have bowed and received Dharma at that moment. It is a pity he was deaf and blind.

In the Diamond Sutra Buddha said, "Subhuti, if a man should declare that the Tathagata is one who comes or goes, sits or lies, he does not understand the meaning of my teaching. Why? The Tathagata does not come from anywhere and does not depart to anywhere; therefore, he is called the Tathagata."

This monk must often have heard a recitation of the Diamond Sutra, but for him the words were without meaning.

GENRŌ:

A white cloud hangs over the summit
Of a green mountain beyond the lake.
Whoever looks and admires the scene,
Need not waste a word.

12. San-shêng Meets a Student

One day, while talking with his monks, San-shêng said, "When a
student comes, I go out to meet him with no purpose of helping him."
His brother monk, Hsing-hua, heard of the remark and said, "When
a student comes, I do not often go out to meet him, but if I do, I will
surely help him."

NYOGEN: Lin-chi, a great Zen master of the T'ang dynasty, passed from the world on the 10th of January, 867. Just before his death he said, "After I am gone, do not destroy my Zen. Keep the teaching among yourselves." San-shêng, who was one of the disciples, asked, "Who would dare to destroy your Zen?" "If anyone asks you what Zen is," Lin-chi inquired, "what do you say?" San-shêng shouted, "Hey!" The teacher was satisfied with the answer and commented, "Who would guess my Zen would be destroyed by this blind donkey?" With these words he died.

Buddhism uses negative words to express reality. It is the only way to avoid the entanglement of words. When Lin-chi said not to destroy his Zen, he was postulating his Zen dualistically, so San-shêng joined him in the same type of expression. Again when the teacher wished to see exactly how it would survive, San-shêng showed him vividly, and the monks gathered there witnessed the immortality of their beloved master. Lin-chi's final words were praise expressed in the negative.

Zen is not a thing that can be given by a teacher to a disciple. The flame of a candle may be put out by the wind, but when conditions are matured, it will burn again, emitting the same light as before. Is it not the same continuous flame after all? San-shêng was not the only one to attain Lin-chi's Zen, but he was brave enough to actualize it in front of his dying teacher. The Zen was his.

As for the kōan of the story, we know that the best help to be gotten from Zen is "no help." Many sects of different religions aim to help people, not realizing that this very help disturbs the inner growth of those so "helped" as well as their own. As sunshine fills the garden, so San-shêng met a student with no thought of giving assistance. Such an admirable mood of tranquil loving-kindness!

Hsing-hua expressed his Zen in the positive, not in contradiction to that of San-shêng but in support of him from the opposite point of view. Positiveness without negativeness may face danger. Negativeness without positiveness causes tardiness. Hsing-hua probably intended to hold the reins of control over the "blind donkey," but I say, "Here, Brother, watch your step. There is a ditch in front of you!"

GENRŌ: One brother says, "No," the other says, "Yes." Thus, they carry the business their father left them, improving it and making it prosper.

The Yellow River runs one thousand miles to the north,
Then turns to the east and flows ceaselessly.
No matter how it bends and turns,
Its water comes from the source in Kun-lun Mountain.

13. Ch'ien-yüan's Paper Screen

Ch'ien-yüan, a master, sat behind a paper screen. A monk came for sanzen, lifted the screen, and greeted the teacher, "It is strange." The teacher gazed at the monk then said, "Do you understand?" "No, I do not understand," the monk replied. "Before the seven Buddhas appeared in the world," said the teacher, "it was the same as the present moment. Why do you not understand?" Later the monk mentioned the incident to Shih-shuang, a Zen teacher of the Dharma family, who

praised Ch'ien-yüan, saying, "Brother Ch'ien-yüan is like a master
archer. He never shot an arrow without hitting the mark."

NYOGEN: In Japan and China people often use a paper screen indoors or outdoors to prevent draughts or as a screen against insects. Ch'ien-yüan must have ordered his monks to come for sanzen as he was using this screen. When I was at the monastery, my teacher often changed his position in the room so that I had to look around for him. The moment my mind jerked, I usually received a blow from his stick. I cannot blame the monk in the story for saying, "It is strange," but Ch'ien-yüan gave him enough time to see the lamp of Dharma clearly inside the screen. Ch'ien-yüan was very kind to give him further instruction.

The Hinayana scripture, Digha Nikaya, mentions seven Buddhas in the world at different times, countless ages before Gautama Buddha. Ch'ien-yüan went back millions of years when he said, "Before the seven Buddhas appeared in the world, it was the same as at the present moment." If the monk had seen his own Buddha-nature, he would have known the reason for his own existence. He had no Zen, despite his teacher's kindness.

In a free translation I made years ago of "Hsin-hsin-ming," a Chinese Zen poem, the last stanzas state: "Zen transcends time and space. Ten thousand years are nothing but a thought after all. What you see is what you have in the world. If your thought transcends time and space, you will know that the smallest thing is large and the largest thing is small, that being is non-being and non-being is being. Without such an experience, you will hesitate to do anything. If you realize that one is many and many are one, your Zen will be complete. Faith and mind-essence are not separated from each other. You will only see 'not two.' The 'not two' is the faith, the 'not two' is the mind-essence. It can only be expressed by silence, but this silence is not the past, this silence is not the present, this silence is not the future."

GENRŌ: Ch'ien-yüan said enough when he gazed at the monk in silence. Shih-shuang should have obliterated the words spoken by Ch'ien-yüan if he considered the good name of his Dharma family.

NYOGEN: We monks are always homeless. We should not have any Dharma family even in the world of teaching. Shih-shuang praised Ch'ien-yüan, but neither of them could teach the monk Zen.

GENRŌ:

Beneath the window midnight rain patters on banana leaves,
On the bank of the river late spring breezes play with the weeping willow.
The message of eternity comes here and there, nothing more, nothing less.
Speaking of seven Buddhas is preparing a rope after the burglar has run away!

14. Pai-yün's Black and White

Pai-yün, a Zen master of the Sung dynasty, wrote a poem:

Where others dwell,
I do not dwell.
Where others go,
I do not go.
This does not mean to refuse
Association with others;
I only want to make
Black and white distinct.

NYOGEN: Buddhists say that sameness without difference is sameness wrongly conceived and difference without sameness is difference wrongly conceived. My teacher, Sōen Shaku, used to illustrate this beautifully, and Dr. D. T. Suzuki has put it into English: "Billows and waves and ripples all surging, swelling and ebbing, yet are they not so many different motions of the eternally self-same body of water?

The moon is serenely shining in the sky, alone in all the heavens and the entire earth; but when she mirrors herself in the brilliant whiteness of evening dew, which appear like glittering pearls sown upon the earth—how wondrously numerous her images! Is not every one of them complete in its own fashion?"

Zen stays neither in assertion nor denial. It is like a steering wheel turning to the left or to the right to guide the vehicle onward. The master in this story was not insisting on his own course, but was warning students not to cling to one side or the other. He sought only to play the game of life fairly even though he knew the fact of non-individuality.

There are many lodges, clubs, and lecture halls, where all sorts of discourses are delivered, each speaker with an urgent message to give to his audience. You can attend these meetings and enjoy the different opinions and arguments, but I advise you to recall occasionally, "Where others dwell, I do not dwell. Where others go, I do not go." It may save you from nervous strain.

The kōan also says, "This does not mean to refuse association with others." We can sympathize with different movements in the world without belonging to any of them. We can welcome visitors from any group and serve them tea, brimful of Zen. Each of you may come and go as you wish. The kōan ends, "I only wanted to make black and white clear." That is to say, we are without color.

15. Ta-t'zu's Inner Culture

Ta-t'zu said to his monks, "Brothers, it is better to dig inwardly one foot than to spread Dharma outwardly ten feet. Your inner culture of one inch is better than your preaching of ten inches." In order to balance and clarify this statement, Tung-shan said, "I preach what I can not meditate, and I meditate what I cannot preach."

NYOGEN: Ta-t'zu, or master Huan-chung (780–862), lived in a

monastery on Ta-t'zu Mountain. Tung-shan was a contemporary twenty-seven years younger. Before you study Tung-shan's saying, you must understand Ta-t'zu's thoroughly. The Mahayana Buddhist wishes to enlighten all sentient beings who suffer from their own ignorance. The motive is great, but he must not forget to cultivate himself minute after minute. He joins the crusade to conquer ignorance and enlighten mankind. The Buddhas and patriarchs of the past and present work with him, and will continue their work in the future. If he misses his step even for a moment, he falls behind.

If one repeats what he hears from others or reads in books, he is not spreading Dharma but adulterating it. In the Orient we call such a person a "three-inch scholar." He reads or hears, then speaks, and the distance from the eyes to the mouth or the ears to the mouth is about three inches. Those who give lectures or write books on Buddhism with no attainment of inward light are working in vain.

A young Greek once asked his comrade on the battlefield what he would do with his unusually short sword. "I will advance one step quicker than the others," came the reply. All he has in the world is that one sword; long or short, he must fight with it. Like the warrior a Zen student has no second thought, therefore, he preaches while he is meditating and meditates while he is preaching. To reach the state of which Tung-shan speaks, one must walk step by step the path Ta-t'zu taught his monks.

16. Kuei-shan's Time

Kuei-shan said to his monks, "Winter repeats its cold days every year. Last year was as cold as this year, and next year we will have the same cold weather. Tell me, monks, what the days of the year are repeating." Yang-shan, the senior disciple, walked to the teacher and stood with his right hand covering the fist of his left on his breast. "I knew you could not answer my question," Kuei-shan commented, then turned to his junior disciple, Hsiang-yen, "What do you say?" "I am sure I can answer your question," Hsiang-yen replied. He walked to his teacher and stood with his right hand covering his left fist placed against his breast as the senior monk had done, but Kuei-shan ignored him. "I am glad the senior could not answer me," was the teacher's remark.

NYOGEN: Kuei-shan's monastery was on a mountain where the monks felt the severe cold of winter. Some of the monks had stayed years in the monastery passing days and months in vain, remembering the cold days of winter, as children think of the Christmas season. Kuei-shan was warning the monks not to waste days with no attainment of Zen.

What is time and when did it begin? When will it end? How do you study Zen? How is your daily Zen in the practical world?

Space and time have been the subjects of philosophical discussion over the ages. Einstein has brought them into the field of mathematics and science.

Time, as experienced by the individual at many periods of his life, is different from physical time, man's invention for use in marking the days. When Yang-shan stood before the teacher with his hands on his breast, he was making a monk's salutation to express his Zen. This was what the days of the year were repeating; he spoke his philosophy in silence.

Past and future are alike to the physicist, differing only in direction as the directions on a compass, but to a living person they are altogether different. A man rolls up his past and carries it with him wherever he goes. When Kuei-shan said, "I knew you could not answer my question," he was merely prodding Yang-shan for being sluggish. He admitted the experience of both disciples, but also showed his own Zen, which was timeless and formless as it flashed.

黄河落天走
東海万里

"No matter how the Yellow River bends and turns, its water comes from the source in Kun-lun Mountain."—From Genrō's poem on Kōan 12, page 35

17. Ta-sui's Turtle

A monk saw a turtle walking in the garden of Ta-sui's monastery and asked the teacher, "All beings cover their bones with flesh and skin. Why does this being cover its flesh and skin with bones?" Ta-sui, the master, took off one of his sandals and covered the turtle with it.

NYOGEN: This monk had the bad habit of jumping to conclusions. He thought if a thing was right at one time, it must be right at all times and in all places. Ta-sui sought to rescue the monk from this type of discrimination and help him to a realization of oneness.

When you see unusual things, you must not be alarmed. First of all, clear away your self-limiting, false conceptions of things and face reality squarely. What is death? What is birth? What is Buddha? What is realization?

Genrō referred to an old poem at the end of his comment; I will translate the whole poem as a conclusion to this story.

GENRŌ:

Friends of my childhood
Are all well known now.
They discuss philosophy;
They write essays and criticisms.
I am getting old;
I am good for nothing.
This evening the rain is my only companion.
I burn incense and lay myself in its fragrance;
I hear the wind passing the bamboo screen at my window.

18. Lin-chi Plants a Pine Tree

One day as Lin-chi was planting a pine tree in the monastery garden, his master, Huang-po, happened along. "We have good shrubbery around the monastery, why do you add this tree?" he asked. "There are two reasons," Lin-chi answered, "first, to beautify the monastery with this evergreen and, second, to make a shelter for monks of the next

generation." Lin-chi then tamped the ground three times with his hoe to
make the tree more secure. "Your self-assertion does not agree with me,"
said Huang-po. Lin-chi ignored his teacher, murmuring, "All done,"
and tamped the ground three times as before. "You will cause my teach-
ing to remain in the world," Huang-po said.

> NYOGEN: Lin-chi was symbolizing his Zen when he planted
> the tree by the monastery, where he had received Dharma,
> but he did not want anyone to notice it until it was old. His
> teacher knew his thought very well, but wished to examine
> him thoroughly, so spoke as though he were inspecting the
> garden of the monastery. Lin-chi replied in kind with no
> reference to Zen. Zen should be preserved in this way. What
> can the teacher say except his words of appreciation?

19. *Chao-chou Plans a Visit*

Chao-chou was planning to visit a mountain temple, when an elder
monk wrote a poem and gave it to him.
Which blue mountain is not a holy place?
Why take cane and visit Ts'ing-liang?
If the golden lion appears in the clouds,
It is not a happy omen at all.
After reading the poem, Chao-chou asked, "What is the true eye?"
The monk made no answer.

> NYOGEN: A Chinese poem of the T'ang dynasty says:
> *All mountains are the temple of Manjusri.*
> *Blue ones afar and green ones near,*
> *Each has the Bodhisattva enshrined.*
> *Why climb Ts'ing-liang mountain?*
> *The sutras depict Manjusri riding a golden lion.*
> *You may see such an illusion in the mountain clouds,*
> *But it is not real to the eye of a Zen student,*
> *It is not the happiness he seeks.*
>
> Genrō praised the monk's poem as well as Chao-chou's
> sharp question. There is a kōan: "Avalokiteçvara has a

thousand eyes. Which one is the true eye?" If you pass this kōan you can also answer Chao-chou's question. The monk might have been answering in silence, but if he liked silence so well, why did he not keep it from the beginning instead of writing a poem? If Chao-chou had a true eye, why did he ask for it? Now, tell me, what is the true eye?

20. Tê-shan Speaks of Preceding Teachers

K'uo was attending his master, Tê-shan, one day when he said, "Old masters and sages, I suppose, have gone somewhere. Will you tell me what became of them?" "I do not know where they are," came the reply. K'uo was disappointed, "I was expecting an answer like a running horse, but I got one like a crawling turtle." Tê-shan remained silent, as one defeated in an argument. The next day Tê-shan took a bath and came to the sitting room, where K'uo served him tea. He patted the monk on the back and asked, "How is the kōan you spoke of yesterday?" "Your Zen is better today," answered the monk. But Tê-shan said nothing, as a man defeated in an argument.

NYOGEN: K'uo asked about preceding masters as some people think of heaven as a sort of glorified world, where those who have died on earth continue their work. As long as he serves his master faithfully, why should he trouble himself with such matters? Although a student may think of his teacher as "master," his teacher does not accept such a title because his Zen is not separate from theirs, and his Dharma is a constituent of their Dharma. Tê-shan was very kind to the monk, whose own Zen was no better than yesterday's dream. "What is the use?" Tê-shan may have thought, but he remained silent.

GENRŌ:

The preceding masters have hearts cold and hard as iron;
No human sentiments can judge them.
They go back and forth like a flash,
Move inwardly and outwardly like magic.

The criticisms of mankind cannot affect them.
One may climb the top of the mountain,
But he cannot search the bottom of the ocean.
Even under a true teacher one must strive hard.
Tê-shan and the monk could not dine at the same table.

21. Fên-yang's Walking Stick

Fên-yang brought forth his walking stick and said to his monks,
"Whoever understands this walking stick thoroughly can end his travel-
ing for Zen."

NYOGEN: Zen monks used to travel by foot, sometimes climb-
ing roadless mountains and crossing unknown rivers, and
they carried long staffs taller than themselves. Fên-yang had
traveled many years in his youth, visiting more than seventy
teachers, so kept his walking stick as a souvenir. In the story
he used the stick to show the monks his Zen. It is not a souvenir. It is not a symbol. What is it? You cannot see it with
your eyes. You cannot hold it with your hands. You cannot
smell it with your nose. You cannot hear it with your ears.
You cannot taste it with your tongue. You cannot form it in
your thought. Here it is!

GENRŌ: All Buddhas in the past, present, and future enter Buddhahood when they understand this walking stick. All gene-
alogical patriarchs reach their attainment through this walking stick. Fên-yang's words are correct; no one can deny
them. I must say, however, that anyone who understands the
walking stick should begin his traveling instead of ending his
journey.
A walking stick seven feet high!
Whoever understands it can swallow the universe.
One goes southward and the other eastward;
Both are within my gate.
Before they leave this gate,
They should end their journey.

Kao-t'ing paid homage to Tê-shan across the river,
Tê-shan answered, waving his fan:
Kao-t'ing was enlightened at that moment.
Hsüan-sha tried to climb the mountain to see his teacher,
But fell down and injured his foot;
At that moment he attained his realization,
And said, "Bodhidharma did not come to China,
And his successor never went to India."

22. Pa-ling's Secret Transmission

A monk asked Pa-ling, "What do the words 'secret transmission in the east and in the west' mean?" "Are you quoting those words from the poem of the third patriarch?" Pa-ling inquired. "No," answered the monk, "those are the words of the master Shih-t'ou." "It is my mistake," Pa-ling apologized. "I am such a dotard."

NYOGEN: Pa-ling was a successor of Yün-mên, the thirteenth patriarch after Bodhidharma. Shih-t'ou was the eighth patriarch, and his poem *San-t'ung-ch'i,* or *Unification,* was well known among the monks, as was the third patriarch's *Hsin-hsin-ming,* or *Faith in Mind.* No monk or teacher would mistake one poem for the other, but Pa-ling wished the words to come from the monk himself, who might then receive the transmission, not in the east or in the west, but at that very moment.

What is the use of your searching books for the sources of various quotations you have heard? When the question is yours, you will find the answer also.

23. Hsüeh-fêng Cuts Trees

Hsüeh-fêng went to the forest to cut trees with his disciple, Chang-shêng. "Do not stop until your ax cuts the very center of the tree," warned the teacher. "I have cut it," the disciple replied. "The old masters transmitted the teaching to their disciples from heart to heart," Hsüeh-

fêng continued, "how about your own case?" Chang-shêng threw his ax to the ground, saying, "Transmitted." The teacher took up his walking stick and struck his beloved disciple.

NYOGEN: Monks are real co-workers, whether meditating in a Zen-dō or working together at daily tasks. There is no doubt these two were carrying the lamp of Dharma. Many Occidentals seek truth, visiting philosophy classes or studying meditation under Oriental teachers, but how many of them cut the tree to the center? They often scratch at the bark, but wait for someone else to split the trunk for them. What mollycoddles!

Chang-shêng attained his Zen before his teacher finished speaking. Hsüeh-fêng was pleased. But after the monk had thrown his ax to the ground, why did he say, "Transmitted?" He deserved his teacher's blow.

GENRŌ:
Chang-shêng had a good ax
Sharp enough to split
The trunk in two
With a single stroke.
Hsüeh-fêng used his walking stick
To sharpen the edge.

24. Nan-ch'üan's Buddhistic Age

Nan-ch'üan once delayed taking his seat in the dining room. Huang-po, his disciple and chief monk, took the master's seat instead of his own. Nan-ch'üan came in and said, "That seat belongs to the oldest monk in this monastery. How old are you in the Buddhistic way?" "My age goes back to the time of the prehistoric Buddha," responded Huang-po. "Then," said Nan-ch'üan, "you are my grandson. Move down." Huang-po gave the seat to the master, but took the place next to it for his own.

NYOGEN: The monks in the monastery were probably clinging to the personality of the master and chief monk. Each monk should keep his own seat and be master of the situation regardless of his age or position, so Huang-po wanted to break this attachment of the monks. A Buddhist counts his age from the date of his ordination, and some monks are very proud of their years. No matter how old the prehistoric Buddha may be, the time is still limiting and finite. Nan-ch'üan lived in eternity without beginning or end, so he told Huang-po to move down. If Huang-po had returned to his own place, it would have been a self-contradiction. Instead he took another seat, and so controlled the situation.

25. Yen-t'ou's Water Pail

Three monks, Hsüeh-fêng, Ch'in-shan, and Yen-t'ou, met in the temple garden. Hsüeh-fêng saw a water pail and pointed to it. Ch'in-shan said, "The water is clear, and the moon reflects its image." "No, no," said Hsüeh-fêng, "it is not water, it is not moon." Yen-t'ou turned over the pail.

NYOGEN: When Hsüeh-fêng pointed to the water pail, he referred to the Buddha-body permeating the world, and Ch'in-shan was in the same mood as the old Buddhist poem:

The moon of Bodhisattva,
Clear and cool,
Floats in the empty sky.
If the mind of a sentient being
Tranquillizes itself
Like a calm lake,
The beautiful image of Bodhi
Appears there in no time.

Hsüeh-fêng emphasized noumenon rather than phenomenon when he said, "It is not water, it is not moon." Yen-t'ou turned over the pail to erase even this denial. Zen is not a philosophy nor a religion.

GENRŌ:

In the garden of willows and flowers
By the tower of beautiful music

Two guests are enjoying wine,
Holding their golden cups
Under the pale light of the moon.
A nightingale starts suddenly
From the branch of a tree,
Shaking dew from the leaves.

FŪGAI: Nightingale? No! It is a phoenix!

26. Hsüeh-fêng's Punctuality

Hsüeh-fêng, the cook monk in Tung-shan's monastery, was always punctual in serving the morning meal. One day Tung-shan asked, "What makes you keep the time so accurately?" "I watch the stars and the moon," Hsüeh-fêng answered. "What if it rains, or is foggy, what do you then?" Tung-shan persisted, but Hsüeh-fêng remained silent.

NYOGEN: In Hsüeh-fêng's time there were no alarm clocks, but the monks arose at four in the morning to meditate an hour or so before the meal. Although Hsüeh-fêng prepared the breakfast before daylight, his gong was always heard on time —neither late nor early. When Tung-shan asked the question, he was praising the cook, and Hsüeh-fêng's reply was smoothly polished without a trace of pride. Lest the other monks misunderstand, Tung-shan asked again, "What if it rains or is foggy?" The monks may have been thinking the cook depended on the stars and moon to keep time. Today we have alarm clocks and other devices to remind us of the hour, but we cannot work accurately and punctually unless we polish our Zen and master situations. We should drive time, not be driven by it. Tung-shan wished Hsüeh-fêng to share his secret with the other monks. Do you think they understood?

GENRŌ: If Tung-shan asked me what I would do if it rained or there was fog, I would answer that I watched the rain and enjoyed the fog.

FŪGAI: I beg your pardon, but I feel like cutting off your tongue with a pair of scissors. Hsüeh-fêng has already answered.

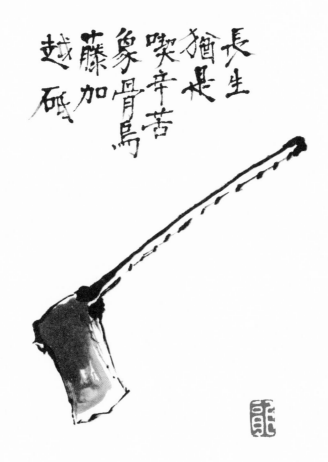

長生
猶是
喫辛苦
象骨烏
藤加
越砥

"Hsüeh-fêng used his walking stick to sharpen
the edge of Chang-shêng's ax."
—From Genrō's poem on Kōan 23, page 48

27. Yang-shan's Million Objects

Yang-shan asked Kuei-shan, "If a million objects come to you, what do you do?" Kuei-shan answered, "A green article is not yellow. A long thing is not short. Each object manages its own fate. Why should I interfere with them?" Yang-shan paid homage with a bow.

NYOGEN: Yang-shan studied Zen under Kuei-shan's guidance, later receiving Dharma and becoming his successor. This anecdote must be one of hundreds that took place during those years of training.

When one postulates and perceives a mental image, it becomes an object to him. Buddhism classifies mental objects with objects of the sensory world. If gladness and sorrow come at the same time, if pleasure and pain gather around him, how should a man manage them? If he has to judge loss and gain, liking and disliking at the same moment, what ought he really to do?

A Zen student should try to do one thing at a time. If you search for an article in your desk, you should push back the drawer that does not serve you and open the next. Each drawer contains something of importance, but if the article is not there, the other things have nothing to do with you at the moment. Would you leave all the drawers open or empty them all on the floor? Yet that is exactly what many people do with their mental objects. Those who eat candy while reading or listen to the radio while writing are likely to stray from the Zen spirit.

28. Lung-ya's Ultimate Stage

A monk asked Lung-ya, "What did old masters attain when they entered the ultimate stage?" "They were like burglars sneaking into a vacant house," came the reply.

NYOGEN: This monk probably thought masters have something others do not have, whereas, they have nothing others have.

Lung-ya's answer may seem awkward, but it was the way to handle this monk. He worked hard at one kōan after another, striving to become a master, and asked about the ultimate kōan as he might about a final examination. He was impatient instead of walking step by step. He could not even dream of the ultimate stage with his disturbed mind, but greedily grabbed anything he came across, so Lung-ya put him in a vacant house.

A healthy person never thinks of sickness, and a sick person struggles to attain health. A man was once asked what he had in him, he looked so calm and contented. In turn he asked the questioner what he had in him, he looked so uneasy and disheartened. One who has nothing in him is always happy, but someone with many desires never gets out of his misery.

GENRŌ:

He walked the blade of a sword;
He stepped on the ice of a frozen river;
He entered the vacant house;
His desire to steal ceased forever.
He returned to his own home,
Saw the beautiful rays of the morning sun,
And watched the moon and stars intimately.
He walked the streets with ease,
Enjoying the gentle breeze.
At last he opened his treasure house.
Until that moment he never dreamed
He had owned those treasures from the very beginning.

29. Yang-shan's Greeting

At the end of seclusion of one hundred days, Yang-shan greeted his teacher, Kuei-shan. "I did not see you around here all summer," said Kuei-shan, "What were you doing?" "I have been cultivating a piece of land," replied Yang-shan, "and produced a basketful of millet." "You

did not pass this summer in vain," Kuei-shan commented. "What were
you doing this summer?" inquired Yang-shan. The old monk answered,
"I ate once a day at noon and slept a few hours after midnight." "Then
you did not pass this summer in vain," Yang-shan responded and with
these words stuck out his tongue. "You should have some self-respect,"
Kuei-shan observed.

NYOGEN: There were fifteen hundred monks in Kuei-shan's monastery, most of them in the Zen-dō meditating day and night, while some took charge of the kitchen and others worked in the fields. Each did his part to glorify Buddha-Dharma. Yang-shan did his part by cultivating a piece of land to produce a basketful of millet, and Kuei-shan led his life as an ideal monk. No one in the whole Zen family passed his summer in vain. From the worldly standpoint this was a scene of greeting between student and master with each appreciating the other, but in Zen the student still showed a trace of his attainment. He lingered in the shadow of gain and loss. He realized his wrong statement before it was ended, but his teacher, recognizing what had been in his mind, scolded him.

GENRŌ:

None of the monks wasted precious time
In the old monastery of Kuei-shan.
Each monk glorified Buddha-Dharma
Working in silence, ignoring loss and gain.
Pet birds have red strings on their legs;
They are still strings, no matter how attractive.
Monks must not be attached to their freedom.
One sticks out his tongue to escape a blow—
Given with loving-kindness—
To sever all strings of mind and body.

30. T'ai-tsung's Dream

Emperor T'ai-tsung of the Sung dynasty one night dreamed of a god who appeared and advised him to arouse his yearning for supreme enlightenment. In the morning His Majesty asked the official priest, "How can I arouse yearning for supreme enlightenment?" The priest said no word.

FŪGAI: His Majesty was still dreaming when he questioned the official priest. The servants should prepare a basin of blue jade, a snow-white cloth, and some icy water to wash his face. The official priest should be dismissed from his post because he failed to assist the emperor to stay awake all the time. When he was asked a question, he said no word, neglected his duty, and was good for nothing.

NYOGEN: The emperor must have been yearning for attainment to have dreamed of it. The priest knew there was no use in answering as long as the emperor knew of nothing beyond dualism, but his silence was not brilliant enough to enter the heart of the dreamer.

GENRŌ: Were I the priest, I would have said, "Your Majesty, you should have asked that question of the god in your dream."

FŪGAI: I wonder if my teacher was ever acquainted with the god of whom the emperor spoke. Even if he were, his advice was too late.

NYOGEN: What is ultimate enlightenment? How does one know that he is yearning for supreme enlightenment? When Buddha attained his realization, he was considering all sentient beings in deep compassion, he sought their welfare and deliverance. Buddha exemplified the true nature of supreme enlightenment. The four-fold vow arouses the yearning and verifies the enlightenment.

31. Kuei-shan Summons Two Official Monks

Master Kuei-shan sent for the treasurer, but when the treasurer monk appeared, Kuei-shan said, "I called the treasurer, not you" The treasurer could not say a word. The master next sent for the chief monk, but when he arrived, Kuei-shan said, "I sent for the chief monk, not you." The chief monk could not say a word.

> NYOGEN: A monastery must have several officers. The treasurer takes care of the funds of the institution and the chief monk looks after all the monks in the Zen-dō. Novices are kept in the Zen-dō to meditate, but old-timers are responsible for different positions in the monastery. Although the two monks in the story had no pride in their positions, they still wanted personal guidance when they presented themselves before their teacher. Kuei-shan detected this dualism and reprimanded them.

32. Fên-yang Punishes the Sky

A monk asked Fên-yang, "If there is no bit of cloud in the sky for ten thousand miles, what do you say about it?" "I would punish the sky with my stick," Fên-yang replied. "Why do you blame the sky?" the monk persisted. "Because," answered Fên-yang, "there is no rain when we should have it and there is no fair weather when we should have it."

> NYOGEN: A Zen monk punishes everything with his big stick; even Buddha and the patriarchs cannot escape that blow of Zen. His stick is the handle by which he can shake the whole universe. If there were to arise any disturbance in the perfect network of the universe, Fên-yang was ready to set things right with his stick. The monk was merely a dreamer expecting to live in uninterrupted bliss while he worshipped a white-washed, dummy Buddha. Fên-yang's first answer was really a warning to the monk, but when he saw the monk did not understand, he simplified his answer as one might to a small child.

33. Yüeh-shan Solves a Monk's Problem

After a lecture to the monks one morning, Yüeh-shan was approached by a monk, who said, "I have a problem. Will you solve it for me?" "I will solve it at the next lecture," Yüeh-shan answered. That evening, when all the monks had gathered in the hall, Yüeh-shan called out loudly, "The monk who told me this morning he had a problem, come up here immediately." As soon as the monk stepped forward to stand in front of the audience, the master left his seat and took hold of the monk roughly. "Look here, monks," he said, "this fellow has a problem." He then pushed the monk aside and returned to his room without giving the evening lecture.

FŪGAI: Why, my dear brother, you have such a treasure for meditation. Without a problem, how can one meditate intensely? Do not ask the help of a master or anyone. The master solved your problem this morning, but you did not realize it. This evening he gives a dramatic lecture, pouring out all he has in his heart.

NYOGEN: What a rice bag! What a splendid lecture! I wonder how many monks of the audience understood it?

Some time ago a priest from Japan visited me in this Zen-dō. "What is Zen," he asked. I put my finger to my lips and whispered, "We do not speak in the meditation room." As he followed me into the library, he was about to ask the same question again, so I put my finger once more to my lips and said, "We read books here in silence." When we reached the kitchen, I did not give him time to ask a question, but said, "We cook here without a word and eat without speaking." As I opened the door and shook hands with him, he gasped, "What is Zen?" and went away.

34. Hsüeh-fêng Sees His Buddha-nature

A monk said to Hsüeh-fêng, "I understand that a person in the stage of Çravaka sees his Buddha-nature as he sees the moon at night, and a person in the stage of Bodhisattva sees his Buddha-nature as he sees the sun at day. Tell me how you see your own Buddha-nature." For answer Hsüeh-fêng gave the monk three blows with his stick. The monk went to another teacher, Yen-t'ou, and asked the same thing. Yen-t'ou slapped the monk three times.

NYOGEN: If a person studies Buddhism to escape the sufferings of the world, he finds that all suffering is caused by his own greed, anger, and ignorance. As he seeks to avoid these three poisons and to purify his heart, he may see his Buddha-nature as beautiful and as remote as a new moon, but most of the time he misses seeing even this. He is in the stage of Çravaka.

Another person studies Buddhism to save all sentient beings. He realizes the true nature of man, and sees Buddha-nature in every person without exception. Cloud, rain, and snow he sees with sadness, but he does not blame the sun, and at night he knows other parts of the earth have bright daylight. He knows that mankind destroys things foolishly, but can also create and build things wisely. He is a Bodhisattva.

The monk's first statements were all right, but if he really understood them, he would know better than to ask Hsüeh-fêng about his Buddha-nature. Hsüeh-fêng tried to bring the monk back from dreamland with his blows, but the monk took his dream to Yen-t'ou, where he received similar treatment. I can imagine his stupid, sleepy face!

35. Li-hsi's Poem

Li-hsi, who lived thirty years on Tzu-hu Mountain, wrote a poem:
For thirty years I have lived on Tzu-hu Mountain.
I have taken simple meals twice a day to feed my body;

I have climbed the hills and returned to my hut to exercise my body.
None of my contemporaries would recognize me.

NYOGEN: As a bird flies freely yet leaves no trace in the air, so the Zen monk should live without making any impression of his passing. Buddha said, "And so because he rests and is at peace within, men revere a monk. Therefore, he ought to avoid all entanglements. For, like a solitary desert tree in which all the birds and monkeys gather, so is a monk who is encumbered much with friends and admirers." Lao-tzu said, "Therefore, in order to avoid opposites, the sage manages his affairs without doing anything, and conveys his instructions without the use of speech. He causes things to happen without acting or claiming ownership or expecting reward; hence, his power is never jeopardized."

The master in our story wished to live in this way. Anyone who accomplishes any great work is indebted to unknown contemporaries. A monk lives on a mountain for thirty years, takes his simple meals and climbs the hills. His life is faultless; he is content. His everyday life constantly preaches Buddhism. What does he care about the recognition of his contemporaries?

GENRŌ:
When inclined, he climbs the mountain;
In his leisure, white clouds are his companions;
In quietude, he has everlasting gladness.
None but Zen students can partake of such pleasure.

36. Where to Meet After Death

Tao-wu paid a visit to his sick brother monk, Yün-yen. "Where can I see you again, if you die and leave only your corpse here?" asked the visitor. "I will meet you in the place where nothing is born and nothing dies," answered the sick monk. Tao-wu was not satisfied with the answer and said, "What you should say is that there is no place in which nothing is born and nothing dies, and that we need not see each other at all."

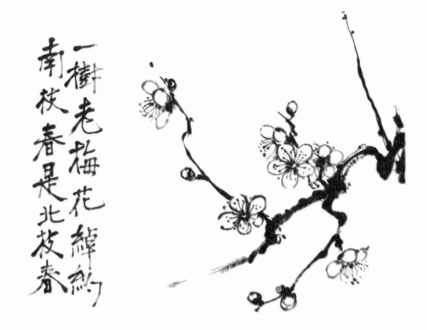

一樹老梅花綽約
南枝春是北枝春

"The southern branch owns the whole spring,
as also does the northern branch."
　　—From Genrō's poem on Kōan 36, page 63

NYOGEN: Both Tao-wu and Yün-yen received the Dharma from Master Yüeh-shan and later became well-known teachers. This anecdote belongs to their youth; at least, they were young in Zen. Tao-wu should not have bothered his sick brother with such a question. We are all constantly approaching death in this world of Anicca (impermanency); the healthy as well as the sick face death daily in a world of Dukkha (discontent). The Buddhist monk realizes the truth of Anatta (egolessness); he never feels Dukkha and lives beyond the world of Anicca.

What impertinence! Why not let the sick monk alone to muse in peace? Since there is no soul that "goes out" at death, if the visitor is not satisfied with a cold corpse, he should look for the warm hand of another living monk and shake it to his heart's content.

The sick monk's answer was not bad, but there is still some trace of postulation. If I had been he, I would have answered, "Do not worry, brother. I shall meditate with you as long as you live." Tao-wu's correction of the monk's reply was nothing but sophistry. Yün-yen should have laughed at him and bid him goodnight.

GENRŌ: Tao-wu loses everything and Yün-yen gains all. The latter said, " I will meet you," and the former said, "We need not see each other at all." They need not see each other, therefore, they meet. They meet each other because there is no need to see each other.

True friendship transcends intimacy or alienation:
Between meeting and not meeting, there is no difference.
On the old plum tree, fully blossomed,
The southern branch owns the whole spring,
As also does the northern branch.

37. Hsüeh-fêng's Sanctity

A monk asked Hsüeh-fêng, "How can one touch sanctity?" Hsüeh-fêng answered, "A mere innocent cannot do it." "If he forgets himself," the monk asked again, "can he touch sanctity?" "He may do so in so far as he is concerned," Hsüeh-fêng replied. "Then," continued the monk, "what happens to him?" "A bee never returns to his abandoned hive," came the answer.

NYOGEN: There is a kōan to illustrate this story. A student asked his teacher, "What is Zen?" "Ts'in," the teacher replied. Ts'in is a Chinese word meaning father, mother, or one's own self when used as a noun; used as an adjective it signifies most intimate or most familiar; and as a verb it means to love, to see constantly, to know well, or to understand thoroughly. The monk in this story aims to touch sanctity as a Sufi looks to his beloved. The monk approaches truth calmly and with empty hands; the Sufi devotes himself piously to his beloved. The monk's attitude is innocent enough, but he must come down out of his ivory tower. The Sufi may sense the beloved, but the true Buddhist makes himself sanctity. Hsüeh-fêng demonstrated his Zen by saying, "A bee never returns to his abandoned hive." Just as the solar constellation traverses the skies, so the mind of a Zen monk goes on from eternity to eternity without clinging to anything.

Psychology observes mental phenomena, and epistemology discusses the theory of knowledge, but these are the shadows of mind and not mind itself. When one finds mind itself, his search ends instantly. He can then "touch sanctity" without any attachment, forgetting all terms, even his selflessness, to become a "bee in the new hive" of freedom. His life is Zen, or "Ts'in."

38. Going and Returning

A monk asked his master, "What do you think of a monk who goes from the monastery and never returns?" The teacher said, "He is an ungrateful ass." The student asked again, "What do you think of a monk who goes out of the monastery, but comes back again?" The teacher said, "He remembers the benefits."

NYOGEN: When a monk enters a monastery, he takes a vow to stay there until he attains realization. If he goes from the monastery, he must have fulfilled himself, in which case he has no business staying there. Zen, however, has no graduates. If a Zen monk thinks he has attained something, he loses his Zen, and his staying in the monastery is then essential.

After being there many years, if he is invited by another monastery to teach, he may go away, but as a rule he ultimately returns to his old nest. Young monks who cannot bear the severity of a Zen teacher leave the monastery. They are ungrateful asses so they never come back to their teacher. If one receives Dharma in a monastery, the master becomes his father and the monastery his home. How can he forget the surroundings which inspired realization? He always remembers the benefits, and returns to his home at the first opportunity.

GENRŌ: If I were asked, "What do you think of a monk who goes from the monastery and never returns?" I would say, "He is a fool!" And on the question, "What do you think of a monk who goes out of the monastery only to return?" I would answer, "He is an escaping fox."

NYOGEN: Genrō gives the monks freedom to come or go as they wish. No master would force the monks to stay in his monastery, but the monk who gives up one teacher and goes to another is usually a fool because he indulges in harsh judgment unfair both to his teacher and to himself.

In this Zen-dō I never consider anyone's coming or going. A frequent visitor may think he belongs here. His idea is all right, but if he stops coming, I do not miss him. A stranger paying a call to this humble house may be disgusted with the quaintness of the surroundings and not come back. I respect his opinion, but he cannot get away from me because my vow is to save all sentient beings, including him. If anyone asks, "What do you think of a friend who stops coming here?" I will answer, "I may see him on the street." And to the question, "What do you think of a friend who comes back to this house?" my reply is, "I will say, 'How do you do? I am pleased to see you.'"

39. Three Calls

Chung-kuo-shih, teacher of the emperor, called to his attendant, "Ying-chên." Ying-chên answered, "Yes." Chung-kuo-shih, to test his pupil, repeated, "Ying-chên." Ying-chên answered, "Yes." Then Chung-kuo-shih called, "Ying-chên," for the third time. Ying-chên answered, "Yes." "I ought to apologize to you for all this calling," said Chung-kuo-shih, "but really you should apologize to me."

NYOGEN: Chung-kuo-shih had stayed in a mountain retreat for forty years, hiding himself from the world, but at last was discovered by the emperor and obliged to have a crowned pupil. At the time of this anecdote the teacher was over one hundred years old, and his disciple, Ying-chên, was a well trained Zen monk, still young, yet able to receive the lamp of Dharma from his teacher. When the teacher called, "Ying-chên," and Ying-chên answered, "Yes," the dialogue of Zen came to an end. Chung-kuo-shih was an old man and wanted to make sure of his pupil's attainment. Ying-chên understood this, so answered patiently. He was expecting his teacher's comment and was happy to hear it. It is a beautiful picture of understanding and harmony.

GENRŌ: The old master was kindhearted enough, and the young pupil served him selflessly. Why the apologies? Because human affairs are very uncertain. One should not set himself in any mold of life if he wishes to live freely.

NYOGEN: When a Zen teacher calls the name of his disciple, he means to knock at the inner door of Buddha-nature. If the teacher has some ordinary business to transact with the disciple, he should not make the call a second time. In Zen neither master nor disciple should waste time, material, words, thought, or energy.

40. *The Dry Creek*

A monk asked Hsüeh-fêng, "When the old creek of Zen dries out and there is not a drop of water left, what can I see there?" Hsüeh-fêng answered, "There is the bottomless water, which you cannot see." The monk asked again, "How can one drink that water?" Hsüeh-fêng replied, "He should not use his mouth to do it."

This monk later went to Chao-chou and related the dialogue. Chao-chou said, "If one cannot drink the water with his mouth, he also cannot take it through his nostrils." The monk then repeated the first question, "When the old creek of Zen dries out and there is not a drop of water, what can I see there?" Chao-chou answered, "The water will taste as bitter as quinine." "What happens to one who drinks that water?" asked the monk. "He will lose his life," came the reply.

When Hsüeh-fêng heard of the dialogue, he paid homage to Chao-chou saying, "Chao-chou is a living Buddha. I should not answer any questions hereafter." From that time on he sent all newcomers to Chao-chou.

NYOGEN: As long as there remains a faint trace of Zen, the creek has not been completely drained. Each person coming here brings his own particular tinge to add to the stream. When Chao-chou referred to losing his life, he meant to lose one's self and enter Nirvana. A person who attempts to become a sage must pass through many difficulties, and even at the last he must quench his thirst with bitterness. If you do not mind these obstacles, I say, "Go to it."

41. *Tung-shan's Tripitaka*

Tung-shan, a Zen master, said, "The Tripitaka, the whole collection of Buddhist scriptures, can be expressed with this one letter." Pai-yün, another master, illustrated the words of Tung-shan with a poem:

Each stroke of the letter is clear, but no reason accompanies it.
Buddha tried to write it, failing many a time.
Why not give the job to Mr. Wang, master of calligraphy?
His skilful hand may accomplish the requirement beautifully.

NYOGEN: The Tripitaka, meaning "Three Baskets" in Sanskrit, contains the Sutra-pitaka or scriptures; the Vinaya-pitaka, the rules and regulations of the brotherhood; and the Abhi-dharma-pitaka, the commentaries on the teachings. At the time of this kōan there were 5,048 volumes comprising the entire text, which Tung-shan says can be expressed with one letter. What is this letter? Do not pay any attention to Pai-yün's, poem. If he meant it as a satire, it is a bad joke on himself.

42. *The Southern Mountain*

Shih-shuang lived on the Southern Mountain and Kuan-ch'i lived on the Northern Mountain. One day a monk came from the Northern Monastery to the Southern Monastery, and Shih-shuang said to him, "My Southern Monastery is not superior to the monastery in the north." The monk did not know what to say, so kept silent. When the monk returned to Kuan-ch'i and told him what Shih-shuang had said, Kuan-ch'i remarked, "You should tell him I am ready to enter Nirvana most any day."

NYOGEN: This monk carried the idea of comparison as he visited one monastery after another. Shih-shuang read it in his face and tried to correct the idea, but the monk was confused and remained silent—a silence that has nothing to do with Zen. Back at his former monastery the gentle master did not scold him, trying instead to indicate oneness without comparison. Man's craving causes suffering, and suffering brings a craving for something else; thus, he never gets out of Samsara, the restlessness of a worldly life. Nirvana extinguishes suffering by destroying craving. Both masters expressed the tranquility of equanimity. We should always be cautious about a person who carries the idea of comparison and wanders from one meeting to another. There is no benefit here for anyone.

43. The Ultimate Truth of Zen

A monk asked Hsüan-sha, "When the old masters preached Dharma wordlessly with a gavel or mosquito brush, were they expressing the ultimate truth of Zen?" Hsüan-sha answered, "No." "Then," continued the monk, "what were they showing?" Hsüan-sha raised his mosquito brush. The monk asked, "What is the ultimate truth of Zen?" "Wait until you attain realization," Hsüan-sha replied.

NYOGEN: The monk was, like many another person, clinging to his own prejudice as the only possible solution. Hsüan-sha sought to alter this idea when he said, "No." The monk could not free himself from a concrete idea, even with the vivid instruction before him. When he asked about the ultimate truth of Zen, he was like a man standing in front of the city hall and asking where the city is. Hsüan-sha gave up and said, "Wait until you attain realization."

GENRŌ: If I were Hsüan-sha, I would throw down the brush instead of making such a luke-warm speech.

FŪGAI: My teacher's words may be good to help Hsüan-sha, but it is a pity he had to use a butcher's knife to carve a chicken.

44. Nan-ch'üan Rejects Both Monk and Layman

A monk came to Nan-ch'üan, stood in front of him, and put both hands to his breast. Nan-ch'üan said, "You are too much of a layman." The monk then placed his hands palm to palm. "You are too much of a monk," said Nan-ch'üan. The monk could not say a word. When another teacher heard of this, he said to his monks, "If I were the monk, I would free my hands and walk away backward."

NYOGEN: When the monk came for sanzen, he meant to express his freedom by not conforming to the rules of entering or leaving the Zen-dō, but Nan-ch'üan's first words jolted him so that he changed his attitude. Where was his freedom then? The world is filled with people who are "too much" of this or that, and there are those who think that by being iconoclastic they can express their freedom. They are all bound. A free person does not display his freedom. He *is* free, so passes almost unnoticed. Since he clings to nothing, rules and regulations never bother him. He may bow or walk backwards; it makes no difference.

GENRŌ: If I were Nan-ch'üan, I would say to the monk, "You are too much of a dumb-bell," and to the master, who said he would free his hands and walk backward, "You are too much of a crazy man." True emancipation has nothing to hold to, no color to be seen, no sound to be heard.

A free man has nothing in his hands.
He never plans anything, but reacts according to others' actions.
Nan-ch'üan was such a skillful teacher
He loosed the noose of the monk's own rope.

NYOGEN: Silas Hubbard once said, "As I grow older, I simplify both my science and my religion. Books mean less to me; prayers mean less; potions, pills and drugs mean less; but peace, friendship, love and a life of usefulness mean more . . . infinitively more."

Here we see a good American who learned Zen naturally in his old age. But why should one wait until he is old?

嗄字經三寫烏焉成馬

"From scribe to scribe the letters change, and likewise does the teaching evolve from hand to hand."
—From a poem by Genrō on Kōan 41

Many people do not know how to free themselves from science and religion. The more they study science, the more they create destructive power. Their religions are mere outer garments too heavy when they walk in the spring breeze. Books are burdens to them and prayers but their beautiful excuses. They consume potions, pills, and drugs, but they do not decrease their sickness physically or mentally. If they really want peace, friendship, love, and a life of usefulness, they must empty their precious bags of dust and illusions to realize the spirit of freedom, the ideal of this country.

45. Yü-ti Asks Buddha

Yü-ti, the premier, asked Master Tao-t'ung, "What is Buddha?"
The master called abruptly, "Your Excellency!" "Yes," answered the
premier innocently. Then the master said, "What else do you search for?"

NYOGEN: Yü-ti collected the various answers of Zen teachers he visited with this question as another person might collect coins or stamps no longer in use. He knew enough of Zen to be able to evaluate some of the answers, but he was quite unprepared for this one; so much so he even forgot why he was facing the master. His "yes" was as simple and natural as a child's reply to his mother's call.

GENRŌ: His Excellency certainly bumped his head on something, but I am not sure whether it was a real Buddha or not.

Do not search for fish in the tree top;
Do not boil bamboo when you return home.
Buddha, Buddha, and Buddha. . . .
A fool holds but a string for coins.

NYOGEN: A Chinese once enjoyed a dish of bamboo sprouts and was told by his host it was cooked bamboo. At home he cut a piece of grown bamboo and cooked it for hours in vain.

In China and Japan people used to carry their coins on a string looped through a hole in the center of the coin. A fool once held the end of the string firmly after the coins had slipped away. Many people still cling to this empty string in the belief they carry the real treasure with them.

46. *The Ideograph for Mind*

An old monk wrote the Chinese ideograph for mind *on the gate, window, and wall of his little house. Fa-yen thought it wrong and corrected it, saying, "The gate must have the letter for* gate, *and the window and wall each its own letter." Hsüan-chüeh said, "The gate shows itself without a letter, so the window and wall need no sign at all."*

NYOGEN: The old monk recognizes the gate, window, and wall as manifestations of mind. He was like Hegel, who saw the world as a great thought-process, with the difference that Hegel wrapped himself in speculation and the monk has freed himself from it. Whereas Hegel's absolute idealism clings somewhat to form in reality, the monk had gone beyond name and thought to dwell in a formless house of which the gate, window, and wall were nothing but mind.

Fa-yen supported the monk in part, but expressed himself differently. He might have said, "I am satisfied with the gate, window, and wall. Why do you label them mind?"

Hsüan-chüeh felt that things showed themselves without names at all.

GENRŌ: I will write the letter "window" on the gate, the letter "wall" on the window, and the letter "gate" on the wall.

NYOGEN: To understand Genrō's statement, you must not only enter the little house where the old monk lived, but let the house enter you.

47. *Chao-chou Measures the Water*

One day Chao-chou visited his brother monk's lecture hall. He stepped up to the platform, still carrying his walking stick, and looked from east to west and from west to east. "What are you doing there?"

asked the brother monk. "I am measuring the water," answered Chao-chou. "There is no water. Not even a drop of it. How can you measure it?" questioned the monk. Chao-chou leaned his stick against the wall and went away.

NYOGEN: A Zen monk carries a long walking stick when he travels, using it to feel out the shallow places if he fords a river. Chu-yü, Chao-chou's brother monk, had just opened his lecture hall to the public, and Chao-chou was anxious to know whether Chu-yü had attained real Zen or not. He carried his walking stick with him as a reminder of their former days together. He felt no atmosphere of attainment as he turned his head from east to west, and would have left his walking stick as a memento even if Chu-yü had not asked what he was doing there. In the Diamond Sutra you will read: "Subhuti, what do you think? Does a Srotapanna think in this wise: 'I have obtained the fruit of Srotapati?'" Subhuti said: "No, World-honored One, he does not. Why? Because while Srotapanna means 'entering the stream,' there is no entering here. He who does not enter a world of form, sound, odor, taste, touch, or quality is called a Srotapanna." Chu-yü had attained non-attainment and said, "There is no water. Not even a drop of it." Chao-chou was happy, leaned his stick against the wall, and went away.

Zen may not add anything to Western culture, but students of Zen will earn non-attainment and in the course of time some modest people with their colorless, soundless influence will produce men and women of higher standards.

48. Ti-ts'ang's Buddhism

One day Ti-ts'ang received one of Pao-fu's disciples as guest and asked him, "How does your teacher instruct you in Buddhism?" "Our teacher," replied the monk, "tells us to shut our eyes and see no evil thing; to cover our ears and hear no evil sound; to stop the activities of our minds and form no wrong idea." "I do not ask you to cover your eyes,"

Ti-ts'ang said, "but you do not see a thing. I do not ask you to cover your ears, but you do not hear a sound. I do not ask you to stop your activities of mind, but you do not form any idea at all."

NYOGEN: This monk was probably very young in both years and Zen. His mind was constantly reaching and clinging to useless and evil things. His own teacher pitied him and gave him a lesson from the Buddhist kindergarten, but since Zen instructions are always given individually, he should have said, "My teacher tells *me*. . . ." Ti-ts'ang's instructions were no doubt too difficult for this youngster. If you have no attachment for a thing you may see, it will simply reflect on your eyes and be gone without leaving a trace on your mind mirror. If you pay no particular attention to what you may hear, no sound will stay with you. Yesterday you may have thought this is right and that is wrong, but today you have not carried the same mind picture from the past to the present. There is nothing to see unless you create your own image. There is no sound to hear unless you make your own record. There is no form of thought unless you build it yourself.

GENRŌ: I do not ask you to shut your eyes. I do not ask you not to shut your eyes. Just tell me what your eyes are. I do not ask you to cover your ears. I do not ask you not to cover your ears. Just tell me what your ears are. I do not ask you to stop your activities of mind I do not ask you not to stop your activities of mind. Just tell me what the mind is.

NYOGEN: Some of you shut your eyes when you meditate. Why don't you also shut your ears? Why don't you also stop your activities of mind? Some of you do not shut your eyes in your meditation. Why don't you hear the sound of no-sound? Why don't you form a thought of no-form?

49. Hsüan-sha's Blank Paper

Hsüan-sha sent a monk to his old teacher, Hsüeh-fêng, with a letter of greeting. Hsüeh-fêng gathered his monks and opened the letter in their presence. The envelope contained nothing but three sheets of blank paper. Hsüeh-fêng showed the paper to the monks, saying, "Do you understand?" There was no answer, and Hsüeh-fêng continued, "My prodigal son writes just what I think." When the messenger monk returned to Hsüan-sha, he told him what had happened at Hsüeh-fêng's monastery. "My old man is in his dotage," said Hsüan-sha.

NYOGEN: Hsüan-sha was an illiterate fisherman until he became a monk and attained Zen under the guidance of Hsüeh-fêng. He was a well-known teacher at the time of this story, and Hsüeh-fêng, proud of him, showed the letter to the monks. The monks had expected to see some beautiful calligraphy, so when Hsüeh-fêng asked if they understood, no one could answer. Hsüeh-fêng said too much as a Zen master when he praised his former student.

Zen is like lightning. No human eye can trace it. When the monks glanced at the blank paper, their lesson for the day was over, so they should have bowed and retired to the meditation hall before their teacher had an opportunity to brag about his prodigal son. The messenger monk was a blockhead. He should have asked for a message of reply, but instead he reported the scene of luke-warm Zen to Hsüan-sha, who had to save the family situation by saying, "My old man is in his dotage." All traces of thought were then wiped away with even the blank paper forgotten.

Today man uses radio and television to send messages all over the world, but because he has no Zen he uses propaganda for selfish purposes, spreading hatred and fear, so that mankind is restless day and night. Is man still a prodigal son of heaven? Is he entering the dotage of old civilization? No, he has simply taken an overdose of sleeping medicine and is stirring from his nightmare.

50. I-chung Preaches Dharma

When master I-chung had taken his seat to preach Dharma, a layman stepped from the audience and walked from east to west in front of the rostrum. A monk then demonstrated his Zen by walking from west to east. "The layman understands Zen," said I-chung, "but the monk does not." The layman approached I-chung saying, "I thank you for your approval," but before the words were ended, he was struck with the master's stick. The monk approached and said, "I implore your instruction," and was also struck with the stick. I-chung then said, "Who is going to conclude this kōan?" No one answered. The question was repeated twice, but there was still no answer from the audience. "Then," said the master, "I will conclude it." He threw his stick to the floor and returned to his room.

NYOGEN: Zen monks preach Dharma intensively. The fewer words, the better. Sometimes a member of the audience asks a question and the teacher answers it, at other times one will approach the teacher and express his attainment. The teacher approves or not and the lesson comes to an end. The teacher is the listener and the listener is the teacher. The whole business concerns everyone present, and no one is exempt from responsibility.

Both layman and monk demonstrated their freedom and should have kept their treasure fearlessly despite the master's words. Fūgai said of the layman, "The morning clouds visit the cave on the mountain." And of the monk, "The evening rain patters on the window of the hut." There is no pretense and no artificiality, so there is freedom. The state of a layman is always "so far so good" to a Zen teacher, but monks are never perfect. I-chung might have said, "Sugar is sweet and pepper is pungent." The layman deserved the blow because he clung to the approval, and the monk because he wished to hurry his attainment. There was no use in enlarging upon the incident, so the audience remained silent.

51. Pao-fu's Temple

One day Pao-fu said to his monks, "When one passes behind the temple, he meets Chang and Li, but he does not see anyone in front of it. Why is this? Which of the two roads is profitable to him?" A monk answered, "Something must be wrong with the sight. There is no profit without seeing." The master scolded the monk, saying, "You stupid, the temple is always like this." The monk said, "If it was not the temple, one should see something." The master said, "I am talking about the temple, and nothing else."

NYOGEN: The temple is reality. When one faces it, he does not see anything. It transcends all discriminations. You may, for example, walk along with a crowd not recognizing anyone and forgetting who you are. This is what Pao-fu refers to as "the front of the temple." But the moment you see an acquaintance, nod and smile, or even stop to greet him, you are walking "behind the temple." If, during your meditation, you create the image of a friend, you are not meditating but dreaming. Master Pao-fu is not scolding you for this, but he is showing you the trick of entering and leaving freely without clinging to either road. His question, "Why is this so?" is the answer. The monk had not entered reality, but had only rationalized about seeing and non-seeing. The monk clung stubbornly to the world of limitation and said, "If it was not the temple, one should see something." He should give up Zen and study law.

Sōen Shaku said, "The world is characterized by mutability and impermanence; those who do not rise above worldliness are tossed up and down in the whirlpool of passion. But those who know the constitution of things see the infinite in the finite and the supraphenomenal in the phenomenal, and are blessed in the midst of suffering and tribulation."

52. Hua-yen Returns to the World of Delusion

A monk asked Hua-yen, "How does an enlightened person return to the world of delusion?" The master replied, "A broken mirror never reflects again, and the fallen flowers never go back to the old branches."

NYOGEN: This monk went beyond his own experience to imagine an enlightened person. Why does he not become enlightened himself, then he will know the answer? Hua-yen's reply can be easily misconstrued. He did not mean to imply that an enlightened person returning to delusion was no longer a noble character; instead, his illustration is an actual phenomenon of the enlightened mind.

Buddha* is the goal of culture, but Bodhisattva is the activity of Buddhahood. To his eye there are not two worlds of delusion and non-delusion, and he lives his life to save all sentient beings. Like the lotus flower, he can bloom in muddy water.

John Galsworthy once said, "A man asked to define the essential characteristics of a gentleman—using the term in its widest sense—would presumably reply, 'The will to put himself in the place of others; the horror of forcing others into positions from which he would himself recoil; the power to do what seems to him to be right, without considering what others may say or think.'"

GENRŌ: To illustrate this story, I shall quote an old Chinese poem:

Look! The evening glow brings up
The stone wall on the lake.
A curling cloud returns to the woods
And swallows the whole village.

---

* "Buddha" as it is used here signifies enlightenment and not Buddha Sakyamuni, the founder of the religion. Buddhism is based on the assumption that all people share the potentiality of becoming Buddha in this life, and only their desire for realization plus their perseverance are required for fulfillment.

"Dialectic and sutra reading will not reveal the teaching; the teaching is like a blind stone turtle in empty space."
    —From a poem by Genrō on Kōan 52

53. Hui-chung Expels His Disciple

Tan-hsia paid a visit to Hui-chung, who was taking a nap at the time. "Is your teacher in?" asked Tan-hsia of an attending disciple. "Yes, he is, but he does not want to see anyone," said the monk. "You are expressing the situation profoundly," Tan-hsia said. "Don't mention it. Even if Buddha comes, my teacher does not want to see him." "You are certainly a good disciple. Your teacher ought to be proud of you," and with these words of praise, Tan-hsia left the temple. When Hui-chung awoke, Tan-yüan, the attending monk, repeated the dialogue. The teacher beat the monk with a stick and drove him from the temple.

NYOGEN: The attending monk was displaying his newly attained Zen on the first occasion that presented itself, instead of keeping it colorless. Tan-hsia took in the situation immediately, and his words should have shamed the monk into silence. Instead, the monk proudly repeated the dialogue to his teacher, who drove him from the temple. The fact that later Tan-yüan succeeded Hui-chung as the national teacher simply proves that no case is hopeless, since all sentient beings have Buddha-nature.

When one thinks he has Zen, he loses it instantly. Why does he not practice the teaching colorlessly and noiselessly?

When Tan-hsia later heard of Hui-chung's rough treatment of the disciple, he said, "Hui-chung justly deserves to be called a national teacher."

54. Yen-t'ou's Two Meals

When Ch'in-shan paid a visit to Yen-t'ou, who was living in quiet seclusion, he asked, "Brother, are you getting two meals regularly?" "The fourth son of the Chang family supports me, and I am very much obliged to him," said Yen-t'ou. "If you do not do your part well, you will be born as an ox in the next life and will have to repay him what you owed him in this life," Ch'in-shan cautioned. Yen-t'ou put his two fists on his forehead, but said nothing. "If you mean horns," said Ch'in-shan, "you must stick out your fingers and put them on top of your head." Before Ch'in-shan finished speaking, Yen-t'ou shouted, "Hey!" Ch'in-shan did not understand what this meant. "If you know something deeper, why don't you explain it to me?" he asked. Yen-t'ou hissed, then said, "You have been studying Buddhism thirty years as I have and you are still wandering around. I have nothing to do with you. Just get out," and with these words he shut the door in Ch'in-shan's face. The fourth son of the Chang family happened to be passing and, out of pity, took Ch'in-shan to his home nearby. "Thirty years ago we were close friends," Ch'in-shan remarked sorrowfully, "but now he has attained something higher than I have, he will not impart it to me." That night Ch'in-shan was unable to sleep and at last got up and went to Yen-t'ou's house. "Brother, please be kind and preach the Dharma for me." Yen-t'ou opened the door and disclosed the teaching. The next morning the visitor returned to his home with happy attainment.

NYOGEN: Ch'in-shan had never declared himself a teacher, but monks gathered around to listen to him, and gradually he came to think he was able to teach others. When he heard about his former friend, Yen-t'ou, living quietly in a remote part of the country, he went to visit him to see if he had everything he needed. Now, in China at that time the eldest son received the best inheritance, and each younger son less and less, so this fourth son could not have had very much even though he gave Yen-t'ou food and shelter. A monk would certainly feel obligation unless he lived his Zen life properly. Yen-t'ou modestly mentioned his "obligation," but his body was Dharmakaya itself and he was living with all the Buddhas and Bodhisattvas. Ch'in-shan could not see this, so he referred to the superstition that a monk, receiving offerings in this life without enlightenment, would work as an ox in the next to repay. Yen-t'ou showed him real life, which was never born and will never die, but fists and forehead have nothing to do with the true shapeless shape; he merely pointed out Dharmakaya with them. Poor Ch'in-shan would not understand, but clung to the illustration of the legend on transmigration even though it was entirely foreign to Buddha's teaching.

His own regret and confusion later brought him to an impasse. When he returned to Yen-t'ou with true heart and empty hands, he was able to receive Dharma. What this was and how it was attained, you can only find out by yourself in your own experience.

55. Mu-chou's Blockhead

When Mu-chou and a strange monk passed each other on the road, Mu-chou called, "Venerable Sir!" The monk turned. "A blockhead," Mu-chou remarked, then each walked on again.

This anecdote was recorded by some monks, and years later Hsüeh-tou criticized it, saying, "The foolish Mu-chou was wrong. Didn't the monk turn? Why should he have been called a blockhead?"

Later Hui-t'ang commented on this criticism, "The foolish Hsüeh-tou was wrong. Didn't the monk turn? Why shouldn't he be called a blockhead?"

NYOGEN: In China monks called each other "Brother," and addressed a stranger as, "Venerable Sir." But no matter what the salutation, it must be expressed in Zen, the brilliancy of one's own true nature. Monks cannot afford to waste time in unnecessary compliments.

When Mu-chou spoke, his thought was his voice and his voice was his thought. If the other monk clung to voice, then he was most certainly a blockhead.

Hsüeh-tou traced the monk's Zen to his action of turning, so he blamed Mu-chou, but Hui-t'ang feared Hsüeh-tou's approval might mislead others. He skilfully wiped the words from the record.

The important part of this kōan is its threat to the reader. He may say that silence is the best answer, but even silence may sometimes be too clumsy an answer to a Zen question.

It is not enough to admire silence, one must live it. When he does, he does not recognize silence. Carlyle once said, "Looking around on the noisy inanity of the world, . . . words with little meaning, actions with little worth, . . . one loves to reflect on the great Empire of Silence, higher than all stars; deeper than the Kingdom of Death! It alone is great; all else is small." Beautiful expression, but he spoke too much and broke the silence.

Wu-tsu said, "When you meet a Zen master on the road, you cannot speak to him, you cannot face him with silence. What are you going to do?" You may speak to Mu-chou if you are not clinging to words. You may face Mu-chou in silence if you are free from silence. If you have Zen, whomever you meet and whatever you see will be your noble and beautiful associate without exception.

56. Lu-tsu Faces the Wall

When monks came for instruction in Zen or laymen came with questions, Lu-tsu would turn his back and face the wall. Nan-ch'üan, his brother monk, criticized this method, "I tell monks to put themselves into the time before Buddha was born in the world, but few of them truly realize my Zen. Merely sitting against the wall like Brother Lu-tsu would never do the monks any good."

NYOGEN: Zen monks are strange fellows. If one says white, then the other says black. They have no intention of contradicting one another. Their purpose is to show a colorless color. Lu-tsu turns his back upon his pupil and faces the wall. Beautiful sermon! But if he does it too often, some monks may imitate his act and pass the counterfeit among the monks in other monasteries. Although Nan-ch'üan warned his monks to avoid such a monotonous method, he was also indirectly supporting Lu-tsu's Zen. Lu-tsu has no other truth than his own family treasure, so why should he not always display it in the same way?

Nan-ch'üan's instruction is also good, and worth more than many thousands of scriptures, but what of holding to time that does not exist? I think if Lu-tsu heard these words, he would turn his back on Nan-ch'üan and face the wall as usual.

GENRŌ: Do you want to meet Lu-tsu? Climb the highest mountain to the point no human being can reach. Do you want to meet Nan-ch'üan? Watch a fallen leaf. Feel the approach of autumn.

The sacred place is not remote;
No special road leads to it.
If one proceeds where a guide has pointed,
He will find only a slippery, moss-covered bridge.

57. *Lin-chi's Titleless Man*

Lin-chi once said to his monks, "A titleless man lives upon flesh and blood, going out or coming in through the gateways of your face. Those who have not witnessed this fact, discover it this minute!" A monk stood up and asked, "Who is a titleless man?" Lin-chi suddenly came down from his chair, seized the monk by the collar of his robe, and exclaimed, "Speak! Speak!" The monk was dumbfounded for a moment, so Lin-chi slapped him. "This titleless man is good for nothing."

NYOGEN: This titleless man is beyond sex, neither male nor female. It is neither being nor non-being. It is neither rich nor poor. It is neither wise nor stupid. It is neither young nor old. It is neither a son of God nor a child of Satan. Lin-chi said that the titleless man lives upon flesh and blood, but don't be cheated by the monk. This titleless man is flesh and blood itself, so do not postulate him beyond that.

We have five gateways in the face: eyes, ears, nose, mouth, and skin. We see form and color with our eyes; hear sounds with our ears; smell odors with our nose; taste flavor with our mouth; and receive sensations with our skin. We think there are five worlds: visual, auditory, olfactory, sapid, and tangible, and broadcast the impression we receive from each, using many names. Lin-chi observes these frivolities as mere tricks of this titleless man, so referred to his coming or going through those gateways. Zen meets this titleless man face to face. Those who meet him once will never forget him. They will accept the validity of Lin-chi's statement without any hesitation.

Lin-chi produced the titleless man in front of the questioning monk, but the monk's Zen was not yet matured. Other monks, watching the titleless monk of this one-act play, appreciated it. Those who fail are martyrs in the history of the teaching, but we can resurrect them at any time. The lamp of Dharma burns forever in all the ten quarters.

58. The Statue of Avalokiteçvara

The people of Korea once commissioned an artist in Cheh-kiang, China, to carve a life-sized wooden statue of Avalokiteçvara. The work was completed, the statue carried to Tsien-t'ang harbor for shipment, when suddenly it seemed to be stuck fast to the beach, and no human power could move it. After negotiations between the Chinese and Koreans, it was decided to keep the statue in China. The statue then returned to its normal weight and was later enshrined at a temple in Ming-chou. A person paid homage to the statue and said, "In the sutra we read that Avalokiteçvara is the possessor of miraculous powers, and in all the lands of the ten quarters there is not a place where he does not manifest himself. Then why is it this holy statue refused to go to Korea?"

NYOGEN: Obviously, the artist produced such an excellent statue the Chinese did not wish to part with it. Superstition and mass psychology accomplished the rest.

Avalokiteçvara symbolizes loving-kindness and wisdom. The artist caught a glimpse of these qualities and expressed them in the statue. Anyone can express them in any medium.

The people of Korea should have used their own culture to make the symbol for themselves.

GENRŌ: Every place is the land of his manifestation, then why should he go particularly to Korea?

NYOGEN: There is a saying in Zen, "A thousand lakes have a thousand images of the moon. If there is no cloud in the sky, the heaven extends itself boundlessly." Many Koreans attained Zen and produced many Avalokiteçvaras as their own symbols.

GENRŌ:

> *One who covers his own eyes*
> *Never sees Avalokiteçvara.*
> *Why does he ask a foreigner*
> *To carve a wooden statue?*
> *The immovable statue on the beach*
> *Is not the true Avalokiteçvara;*
> *The enshrined statue in the temple*
> *Is not the true Avalokiteçvara.*
> *The empty ship returns to Korea,*
> *But the man who opens his eyes. . .*
> *Is he not a true Avalokiteçvara?*

59. *Wu-yeh's Fancies*

Wu-yeh, a national teacher, said, "If one has fancies about sages or mediocrities, even though these fancies are as fine as delicate threads, they are strong enough to pull him down into the animal kingdom."

NYOGEN: Wu-yeh, one of Ma-tsu's successors, was at one time the emperor's teacher. His real name was Ta-t'a, but he is known in the records as Wu-yeh, the name given him by the emperor, meaning "no karma." When anyone came to him for personal guidance, he would say, "Do not nurture any fancies, whether good or bad, whether of sages or mediocrities," or, "When you are about to die, if you cannot cut the delicate threads of fancies of sages and mediocrities, you will probably be born as a donkey or a horse in your next life." Genrō did not like this remark concerning transmigration, so changed it to read as we have it now. Zen has no idea of an individual soul crossing a line between this life and the next, or of human life and animal life. From one minute to the next you are always about to die. When you create a fancy, you are likely to go down but never come up.

If you drop a coin into a calm pool, the ripples increase one after another, and it makes no difference whether the coin is gold or copper. The moment the sea of our mind raises a ripple, the calmness is disturbed and the peace broken. Wu-yeh may have had an idea of "no karma," but it would be a mere stone Buddha of motionlessness.

FŪGAI: Why do you refuse the idea of sages and mediocrities? Why are you afraid of being pulled down to lower stages? A good actor never chooses between the roles. The poor one always complains of his part.

GENRŌ: If you want to clear both ideas of sages and mediocrities, you must make yourselves donkeys and horses. Do not hate enemies if you want to conquer them.

Sages and mediocrities . . .
Donkeys and horses . . .
All of them pull you down
When you hold
Even to the shadow of a single hair.
Be good, monks,
Live one life at a time
Without dualistic inertia.
Old masters know your sickness
And shed tears for you.

When asked how to obtain Buddhahood, Nan-ch'üan picked up a tile and began polishing it as though to make a mirror. —From a comment on Kōan 52

60. The Wooden Pillow

In Nan-ch'üan's monastery the cook monk was entertaining the gardener monk one day. While they were eating, they heard a bird sing. The gardener monk tapped his wooden arm-rest with his finger, then the bird sang again. The gardener monk repeated this action, but the bird sang no more. "Do you understand?" asked the monk. "No," answered the cook monk, "I do not understand." The other monk struck the pillow for the third time.

NYOGEN: In a monastery the gardener monk raises vegetables for the cook monk, and they are naturally intimate and friendly. The bird sang because nature inspired him to sing. The gardener monk knew how to enter the mood of these mountain dwellers; thus, his first tap brought the song again. But when he tapped the pillow for the second time, the bird had already flown away. The cook monk lives in a world of desires; he has to think of the mouths and stomachs of other monks. When the monk tapped the pillow the third time, delivering a message from nature, there still remained one pair of ears spiritually deaf.

GENRŌ: Birds sing naturally; the gardener monk taps the pillow innocently. That is all. Why doesn't the cook monk understand? Because he has something in his mind.

61. Yün-mên's Holy Fruits

Yün-mên once lived in a temple called the "Chapel of Holy Trees." One morning a government official called on him and asked, "Are your holy fruits well ripened now?" "None of them was ever called green by anyone," answered Yün-mên.

NYOGEN: It takes three years to see the first fruit of the peach tree, and eight years for the persimmon. The trees called "holy" must have grown in the temple yard. The Chinese officer knew that the name of the trees merely indicated the fruit of wisdom and wanted to see Yün-mên's Zen actualized that moment. He did not want to wait three years or eight years. Neither did he want to linger in memory of Old Buddha. Yün-mên's answer showed the fruit of Zen. The knowledge of cognition may be obtained gradually as one watches it turn from green to red, but Zen realization comes forth with mature form and ripe color.

GENRŌ: His Zen is not ripened. His words are luke warm.

FŪGAI: I love that green fruit.

NYOGEN: This Zen-dō, according to the name, must have some Zen. When you are asked what kind of Zen you obtain here, how do you answer the question? We did not carry our Zen with us when we moved to this dwelling. We did not leave it behind in our former abode. We did not divide it among us, each slipping a small piece into his pocket. When we turn on the lamp and burn a stick of incense, our Zen flares up filling the room from floor to ceiling and saturating it to each corner. Pay homage to the questioner or shake hands with him. It does not matter whether the question is wise or foolish. He also has Zen which no one calls green.

GENRŌ:

The rootless holy tree
Bears holy fruit.
How many are there?
One, two, three. . . .
They are not red;
They are not green.
Help yourself;
They are hard as iron balls.
When the Chinese officer tried to bite
Yün-mên's fruit of the Holy Chapel,
He lost his teeth in them.
He did not know the size was great enough
To cover heaven and earth,
And contain all sentient beings.

62. Nan-ch'üan's Little Hut

One day, while Nan-ch'üan was living in a little hut in the mountains, a strange monk visited him just as he was preparing to go to his work in the fields. Nan-ch'üan welcomed him, saying, "Please make yourself at home. Cook anything you like for your lunch, then bring some of the left-over food to me along the road leading nowhere but to my work place." Nan-ch'üan worked hard until evening and came home very hungry. The stranger had cooked and enjoyed a good meal by himself, then thrown away all provisions and broken all utensils. Nan-ch'üan found the monk sleeping peacefully in the empty hut, but when he stretched his own tired body beside the stranger's, the latter got up and went away. Years later Nan-ch'üan told the anecdote to his disciples with the comment, "He was such a good monk, I miss him even now."

NYOGEN: Nan-ch'üan must have been enjoying his solitude, forming a sort of Zen of his own. The monk wished him to free himself from all forms of ideas, but knew his argument would never convince Nan-ch'üan. Nan-ch'üan realized what the monk was trying to show him, so lay down to sleep in the empty hut, but emptiness is not the true home for a Zen monk. The stranger went away leaving Nan-ch'üan in the new world of creativeness.

Zen takes food from a hungry man and the sword from a soldier. Anything to which one attaches himself most is the real cause of suffering. The strange monk wished to give Nan-ch'üan nothing but true emancipation. Later, when Nan-ch'üan told his disciples how he missed the old pilferer, he must have been enjoying his real emancipation in everlasting gratitude to this unnamed teacher.

63. Yüeh-shan's Lecture

Yüeh-shan had not delivered a lecture to his monks for some time, and at last the chief monk came to him and said, "The monks miss your lecture."

"Then ring the calling-bell," said Yüeh-shan.

When all the monks were gathered in the lecture hall, Yüeh-shan returned to his room without a word. The chief monk followed him, "You said you would give a lecture. Why don't you do it?" "Lectures on sutras should be given by scholars of the sutras, and those on shastras by students of the shastras. Why do you bother this old monk?"

NYOGEN: A Zen teacher exemplifies what the sutras teach, and shastras are commentaries on the scriptures. If one can live as Buddha taught, sutras and shastras mean nothing to him. Yüeh-shan gave lectures for beginners—a finger pointing to the moon—but from morning to night and night to morning his living was a constant lecture to the monks. This lecture was the real one. If some monks overlook this wordless teaching, they are not fit to study Zen. The chief monk deserves thirty blows.

When Tê-shan gained an insight into the truth of Zen, he immediately took up all his commentaries on the Diamond Sutra, which he had once considered invaluable and indispensable, and threw them into the fire. When they were reduced to ashes, he said, "However deep your knowledge of absolute philosophy, it is like a piece of hair placed in the vastness of space; and however important your experience in things worldly, it is like a drop of water thrown into an unfathomable abyss."

Kosen Imakita, teacher of Sōen Shaku, said, "Even a million volumes of scripture are the light of a candle to the sun when you compare them to the actual experience of enlightenment." I do not mean to discourage your study of Buddhism through books. The Occident needs scholars of sutras and shastras these days. It also urgently needs a constant practitioner of Zen like Yüeh-shan.

GENRŌ:

Yüeh-shan's Zen
Is like a full moon,
Whose pale light penetrates

Thousands of miles.
Foolish ones cover their eyes
Overlooking the truth of Zen.
A bell calls the monks;
The old teacher retires to his room.
What a beautiful picture of Zen!
What a profound lecture on Zen!

64. Ching-ch'ing's Big Stick

Ching-ch'ing asked a new monk from whence he had come. The monk replied, "From Three Mountains." Ching-ch'ing then asked, "Where did you spend your last seclusion?" "At Five Mountains," answered the monk. "I will give you thirty blows with the big stick," said Ching-ch'ing. "Why have I deserved them?" questioned the monk. "Because you left one monastery and went to another."

NYOGEN: When a new monk meets the teacher of the monastery, he is usually asked where he has come from. The monk in this story thought it unnecessary to give this information as it was no one's business but his own. His replies, "Three Mountains," and "Five Mountains," meant places regardless of name. A monk must stay in a monastery from April 15th to July 15th, secluding himself in meditation. Between July 15th and October 15th he is free to travel wherever he wishes to select the place for his next seclusion between October 15th and January 15th of the succeeding year. He is then free to come and go as he wishes until April 15th.

This monk was an honest person, no doubt obedient to these rules. He thought he was free to wander as he wished as long as he kept the precepts, but after all, he happened to be a monk, not a vagabond. Our names are merely to identify one another, but once a person makes himself a certain name, he must stick to it. No nameless person exists, just as there is no nameless place when it comes under comparison. Was not this monk clinging to an imaginary freedom? Although his teaching aimed at the achievement of absolute emancipation, Bodhidharma was very severe in the regulation of his students.

65. The Most Wonderful Thing

A monk came to Pai-chang and asked, "What is the most wonderful thing in the world?" "I sit on top of this mountain," answered Pai-chang. The monk paid homage to the teacher folding his hands palm to palm. At that moment Pai-chang hit the monk with his stick.

NYOGEN: The monk came to Pai-chang expecting to hear some unusual teaching or to witness a miraculous phenomenon, but Pai-chang received him in an empty room with the casual observation, "I sit on top of this mountain." Is it not the most wonderful thing in the world? In the *Shōdō-ka,* or *Song of Realization,* Yōka-daishi says, "The Tathagata is interviewed when one enters upon a realm of no-form." The monk bowed to the living Buddha, folding his hands palm to palm, but at the same moment Pai-chang hit him with a stick to crush the image.

From the top of a mountain come the words, "The ignorant cherish the idea of rest and unrest, whereas the enlightened have no likes and dislikes. All forms of dualism are contrived by the ignorant themselves. They are like visions of flowers in the air. Why should we trouble ourselves to take hold of them? Gain and loss, right and wrong; away with them once and for all." Congratulations to you!

66. Tao-wu's Greatest Depth

Tao-wu was sitting on the high seat of meditation when a monk came and asked, "What is the greatest depth of the teaching?" Tao-wu came down from the seat to kneel on the floor saying, "You are here after traveling from afar, but I am sorry to have nothing to answer you."

FŪGAI: Look out, brother! You are endangering yourself in the deep sea.

NYOGEN: Yes, it is true. This monk does not realize his danger even though he is on the verge of drowning. The entire atmosphere of Tao-wu's monastery is the greatest depth of Zen, but the monk postulates it as a thing apart. Why does he not join the group in meditation? At first he may not see anything, but gradually the mists of delusion will melt in the warmth of the sun. The teacher is very kind, but since the teaching is neither high nor low, has neither surface nor bottom, there is nothing to show the monk.

GENRŌ: I should say that Tao-wu certainly had the greatest depth of his Zen.

FŪGAI: I should say that my teacher knows the depth of Tao-wu's Zen.

NYOGEN: Such family gossip makes me blush! I wish no one had said a thing from the beginning.

GENRŌ:
The great and deep sea!
No boundry in four directions!
When Tao-wu comes down
From his high seat,
There is no depth. . . .
There is no water.

FŪGAI:
It is beyond great and small;
It is above shallow and deep.
I fear my beloved teacher
Is in danger of drowning
Because he has a big heart
And loves all sentient beings.

67. Ch'ien-fêng's Transmigration

Ch'ien-fêng asked, "What kind of eyes do they have who have trans-migrated in the five worlds?"

NYOGEN: Hakuin, in his *Zazen Wasan,* or *Song of Meditation,* said, "The reason we transmigrate through the five worlds is because we are lost in the darkness of ignorance." Originally, in India the five worlds were classified as psychological stages, but in the early translations China mistook the names as representing individuals living in five different worlds. Briefly, the five worlds are these: Manusya, normal condition of mind, human stage; Asura, when we lose our balance in feelings and desires; Tiryagyoni, animal mind, when intellectual power vanishes and five senses rule; Preta, the hungry devil; Naraka, suffering devil. Ch'ien-fêng gave his monks this question in an effort to crush their delusions.

FŪGAI: What kind of eyes do those have who do not transmigrate?

NYOGEN: One may have a lovely smile in the morning and an angry face in the evening, traveling from the human stage to the Tiryagyoni stage in a day. His eye was filled with kindliness in the morning and hate in the evening, but Zen does not discuss this kind of eye at all. "The eye with which I see God is the very eye with which God sees me."* "Then," you say, "there must be two kinds of eyes." No! No! Even thousand-eyed Avalokiteçvara has only one true eye. Ignorant persons are cheated by illusions, but sages know how to enter other stages to save suffering beings. A Bodhisattva should have no fear of passing through the battlefield or walking hand in hand with Preta to the bottom of the land of Naraka.

GENRŌ:

The whole world is my garden.
Birds sing my song;
Winds blow as my breath;

* Meister Eckhart (Johannes), *c.* 1260–1327

乾坤渾遇
齒牙塞

*"He did not know the size of Yün-mên's fruit
was great enough to cover heaven and earth."*
 —From Genrō's poem on Kōan 61, page 94

The dancing of the monkey is mine;
The swimming fish expresses my freedom;
The evening moon is reflected
In one thousand lakes,
Yet when the mountain hides the moon,
All images will be gone
With no shadow remaining on the water.
I love each flower representing spring
And each colorful leaf of autumn.
Welcome the happy transmigration!

68. *Yün-mên's Three Days*

Yün-mên said to his monks one day, "There is a saying, 'Three days can make a different person.' What about you?" Before anyone could answer, he said quietly, "One thousand."

NYOGEN: This saying was popular among the Chinese literati from the third century A.D., allegedly coming from a military officer whose aide was most stupid. The officer once suggested the stupid one read more books. Not long afterward the officer was away on official business, and on his return found his aide no longer stupid, but with altered opinion and greater information, gained during the separation. The officer was greatly pleased and praised the aide saying, "Three days can make a different person."

Paderewski once remarked, "If I do not practice for one day, I can tell the difference; if I do not practice for two days, my critics can tell the difference; if I do not practice for three days, everyone can tell the difference."

The number of days has nothing to do with the kōan. At that moment some of the monks under Yün-mên may have been proud of their advancement in Zen during seclusion, and others may have been ashamed of their tardy meditation despite the number of years they had been with Yün-mên. When Yün-mên said, "One thousand," he also did not refer to time nor number. He was a Kegon scholar leaning to the philosophy that one minute contains a thousand years and a thousand years are nothing but one minute. His answer may have been more instructive than encouraging.

FŪGAI: If I were there, I would slap Yün-mên's cheek. Not three days; every inhalation and exhalation may change a person. (Then, after Yün-mên's "One thousand.") Yün-mên has the same old face.

NYOGEN: If I were there at the time, I could rise and bow to Yün-mên, offering the old teacher best wishes for longevity.

GENRŌ: Yün-mên opened a bargain sale and bought himself, so there is no loss and no gain. No one can price his, "One thousand." I would rather say, "It is all right for his time, but it is not all right today." Can you not see that three days alter a person?

NYOGEN: A school teacher always welcomes former pupils, whether they have become great scholars or prosperous businessmen. From the beginning he has known the pupils are not rivals, but that they will later give him credit for his part in their training. Zen teachers, who may be inclined to discredit former colleagues in the old monastery, should meditate on this kōan again and again.

69. The Government Official

Chên-ts'ao, government official, went upstairs with some of the members of his staff. On seeing a group of monks passing below in the road, one of the men said, "Are they traveling monks?" Chên-ts'ao answered, "No." "How do you know they are not traveling monks?" the staff member asked. "Let us examine them," Chên-ts'ao replied, then shouted, "Hey! monks!" At the sound of his voice they all looked up at the window. "There!" said Chên-ts'ao, "didn't I tell you so?"

NYOGEN: Chên-ts'ao was a senior Zen student as well as a high official, whereas his lesser officials were new students in Zen. He wished to instruct them in Zen, so carried this dialogue to that end. This incident took place in a monastery rather than a government building, so the anecdote refers to Zen and nothing else. One of the officials recognized the passing monks with his discriminating mind, deserving a rebuke at that moment. Chên-ts'ao's "no" denied myriad discriminations with the everlasting no; his subordinate argued only as to the superficial identity of the travelers. Were I Chên-ts'ao, I would again say, "No," but Chên-ts'ao was kind and said, "Let us examine them." When the monks looked up at his shout, the under-official may have thought, "Didn't I tell you so?" It was to remove this idea that Chên-ts'ao said, "There! Didn't I tell you so?"

GENRŌ: Chên-ts'ao was looking southeast while his mind was northwest.

NYOGEN: One day Sōen Shaku received a noted newspaperman as his guest. While they had tea, Sōen Shaku talked of politics and world conditions until at last the guest said, "I know all about these things. I came here to learn Zen. Please tell me about it." Sōen Shaku quietly replied, "That is what I have been doing." The newspaperman then understood his own work and, receiving sanzen morning and evening, developed the quality of mind that transcends worldly affairs.

Years ago I kept seclusion in a Seattle hotel room, receiving visitors to join my meditation, when one day a drunkard came in and said, "I understand that Zen monks shout 'Katz!' I want to hear it from you." "You are not qualified to enter meditation when you have liquor in you," I answered him. "Please step out."

The next day he came again, joined the meditation and continued through the week. We did not speak, but meditated together. The next year I returned to the same hotel, and once again he appeared. This time we visited and studied together. I gave him the name Kotō, meaning "Old Lamp." Then several years passed with no further word until I read of his death in the newspaper. The article said he had been in charge of a sawmill and had died during a fire as he fought to save some equipment. His company honored him in death, and I folded my hands palm to palm saying, "The Old Lamp still burns." I never showed him the imitation "Katz," and he never again asked for it.

70. *Chao-chou's Dwelling Place*

One day Chao-chou visited Yün-chü, who said, "Why do you not settle down in your old age?" "Where is the place for me?" asked Chao-chou. "The ruins of an old temple are here on the mountain," Yün-chü suggested. "Then why don't you live there?" Chao-chou asked. Yün-chü did not answer. Later Chao-chou visited Chu-yü, who asked, "Why do you not settle down in your old age?" "Where is the place for me?" questioned Chao-chou as before. "Don't you know your own place for your old age?" Chu-yü countered. Chao-chou then said, "I have practiced horseback riding for thirty years, but today I fell from a donkey."

NYOGEN: Chao-chou went to visit one teacher after another when he was sixty years old, and was still traveling as a wandering monk when he was eighty. His Zen was as ripe and mellow as old wine, but some monks or teachers may have thought it still unseasoned. When Yün-chü suggested that he settle down, Chao-chou knew his own true home and that no place lay outside it, so his response, "Where is the place for me?" was ironic. Chao-chou, perceiving Yün-chü's lack of complete understanding in clinging to his first impression, suggested Yün-chü live among the ruins himself. Yün-chü's silence admitted Chao-chou's attainment.

Chu-yü asked Chao-chou the same question for the same reason, and Chao-chou's repeated response gave Chu-yü room to display his understanding. Chao-chou, who had mastered a high-spirited horse, now found a donkey could not carry him. Chu-yü understood Chao-chou even less than Yün-chü.

Chao-chou later lived in a temple, taught many monks, and attained his full age of one hundred and twenty years. He used neither the "big stick" nor the harsh voice of other masters, but the few words he spoke brimmed with Zen.

Zen teachers in China and Japan lived in historic temples or monasteries supported by the nobility. Stupid monks clung to the splendor and fame of these temporal abodes without regard for a teacher's attainment. Chao-chou freed himself from these false standards when he examined the understanding of established teachers as he wandered. It is almost to be regretted that he later lived in a temple rather than continuing to float as a cloud in the sky. Among Buddhists in the world are those who hide their attainment yet influence people as did the Sufi teachers, Rinds or Dervishes.

71. Yün-mên's Family Tradition

A monk asked Yün-mên, "What is your family tradition?" Yün-mên answered, "Can you not hear the students coming to this house to learn reading and writing?"

NYOGEN: Each Zen teacher has his own way of receiving Zen students. Hakuin's successors in Japan received students one by one, examining the understanding of each on his kōan. Dokuon would continue to smoke as the student entered his sanzen room, smile at him without a word or suddenly laugh when the student expressed his view of the kōan, then ring the bell for him to retire before the student could make a second bow. Kando kept a stick in front of his seat and would say to the student, "Come nearer. I am getting old and hard of hearing." When the student was within reach, Kando would hit him with the stick. Once I experienced his family tradition during sanzen, so next time, when he asked me to come nearer, I approached near enough to hold the stick as I expressed my opinion of the kōan. Sōen Shaku often changed the position of his seat, especially at evening, so the student would not see him immediately.

In Yün-mên's time there was no set method of receiving

sanzen. Monks approached him whenever the opportunity offered: in the garden, in the corridor, or even during his bath. This story took place near the outer gate, where children were passing on their way to school. Yün-mên received all people in the world as his students, even children in grade school were beginning to receive his guidance although they neither saw nor knew him. Here he shows his Kegon philosophy: One is many and many are one.

If you read the dialogues of Zen from the T'ang or Sung dynasties, you will find personal guidance was given after the lecture was over to those who stepped up and asked a question. Buddha, according to the scriptures, also taught this way, but when the teaching was brought to Japan, this method gradually became a part of ceremony or ritual, causing vanity and ambition among the students, who tried to corner the teacher or create a scene. It was like a cheap road show. It was to avoid this condition that Hakuin began the practice of forcing each student to come to his room alone, morning and evening, whether he had reached an opinion or not. But this in turn also became a ceremony with students concerned about failing or passing as in school examinations. It is far from Zen thought.

In Yün-mên's time the Confucianists offered the common education, stressing morality more than learning. Yün-mên purposely emphasized the ethical point to inspire the monk to keep the precepts daily before postulating trascendental philosophy.

GENRŌ: Yün-mên would not get many students in this way as most of them came to gather attractive family traditions.

FŪGAI: Probably Yün-mên has nothing to do but take the place of a school teacher.

NYOGEN: If a Zen monk has nothing to do but take the place of a school teacher, he is an ideal Zen monk. He need not conceal his family tradition in order to attract wandering monks.

72. Pao-shou Turns His Back

Chao-chou visited Pao-shou, who happened to see him coming and turned his back. Chao-chou spread the mat he carried to make a bow to Pao-shou, but Pao-shou immediately stood up and returned to his room. Chao-chou picked up his mat and left.

NYOGEN: In India a monk has his outer clothing, his underclothing and a mat he uses as a blanket at night or a seat in the daytime. Although this mat was sufficient for the climate of India and Ceylon, it became a formal symbol for the monks in the cold of northern China.

Pao-shou's Zen was refined. He made himself like a crystal ball with neither back nor front. Chao-chou recognized it and prepared to pay homage, whereat Pao-shou immediately left because there was no necessity to observe the outer convention of their heart-to-heart understanding. Then Chao-chou also left.

When Han-shan received a monk from another monastery, he asked, "Where are you from?" The monk named his monastery. "What did you learn there?" asked Han-shan. "Meditation," the monk replied. "Show me how you meditate," Han-shan directed. The monk responded by sitting up in the cross-legged position of a Buddhist statue. Han-shan shouted at him, "Hey! You stupid one! Get out! We have enough stone Buddhas in our temple."

This monk has a separate back and front. When he meditates, he looks like a stone Buddha, but when he eats, he is like Preta, and sometimes he may resemble Asura. No wonder Han-shan did not want him to stay in his monastery. "But," you may ask, "did not the teacher ask to be shown how the monk meditated?" The monk who really meditates never sits, never stands, never lies down, and never speaks. Now, what is the proper way to demonstrate meditation? But you must not imitate either Pao-shou or Chao-chou.

73. Hsüeh-fêng Rejects a Monk

A monk came to Hsüeh-fêng and made a formal bow.

FŪGAI: He is using the first lesson for children.

NYOGEN: Does he mean to call the monk a beginner or is he considering the meeting formally begun?

Hsüeh-fêng hit the monk five blows with the stick.

FŪGAI: Here the kōan flares up.

At this the monk asked, "Where is my fault?"

FŪGAI: You do not know your own benefactor.

With another five blows the master shouted at the monk to get out.

FŪGAI: Too much kindness spoils a child.

NYOGEN: Chinese children are first taught a sentence of simple characters that reads, "The ancient great sage, Kung-fu-tzu, had three thousand pupils, among them were seventy good ones. You little boys of eight or nine years should learn to be polite to each other." This is like the A-B-C of English. The monk was very polite to begin with, but Hsüeh-fêng saw him as a beginner in Zen, as Fūgai's comment indicates. Those who study deeply should also bow when they first meet their teacher. The monk's only fault was a sort of momentary stage fright, which deserves a blow. Had he realized this, the monk would not have asked where his fault was. Certainly, he does not know the real benefactor standing in front of his nose. He should bow again before Hsüeh-fêng chases him out.

GENRŌ: Hsüeh-fêng's last shout had no value at all.

FŪGAI: Hsüeh-fêng tried to fit a square stick to a round hole.

NYOGEN: I do not believe that Hsüeh-fêng shouted at all. Whoever described this story did not know colloquial Chinese. In modern Chinese the last sentence of this kōan should be read without putting any meaning to "Katz," although the followers of Lin-chi seem to consider this an indispensable expression.

放
出
葉
月
山
一
團

"Yüeh-shan's Zen is like a full moon."
—From Genrō's poem on Kōan 63, page 96

GENRŌ:
> *Hsüeh-fêng's Zen was like a grandmother's kindness.*
> *He marked the ship's side for a lost sword.*
> *It is like the old story of Lin-chi,*
> *Who poked Ta-yü's ribs three times.*

NYOGEN: A foolish man dropped his sword overboard one day, then carefully marked the ship's side to show the captain where the search should begin without realizing the ship was sailing along. Professors who lecture their classes on the old philosophies with no due allowance for mankind's progress over the years are in effect trying to find a lost sword from a mark on the ship's side.

Lin-chi asked Huang-po what the significance of Buddhism was, and received in reply a blow from Huang-po's stick. Twice again Lin-chi came with the same question and received the same answer. Almost ready to give up his search, Lin-chi went to Ta-yü to complain about his failure. At hearing the story Ta-yü said, "Huang-po was almost too kind. You are such a fool you cannot see." Before Ta-yü finished his remark, realization came to Lin-chi like a flash. Lin-chi poked Ta-yü's ribs three times with his fist.

This poem also marks the ship's side. No wonder Fūgai said, after the last line of the poem, "You cannot catch a rabbit in the same hole twice."

74. The Founder of a Monastery is Selected

While Kuei-shan was studying Zen under Pai-chang, he worked as a cook for the monastery.

FŪGAI: A peaceful Zen family!

Ssu-ma T'ou-t'o came to the monastery to tell Pai-chang he had found a good site for a monastery on the mountain of Ta-kuei-shan, and wished to select a new master before the monastery was established.

FŪGAI: Who could not be the dweller?

Pai-chang asked, "How about me?"

FŪGAI: Do not joke!

Ssu-ma T'ou-t'o replied, "That mountain is destined to have a prosperous monastery. You are born to poverty, so, if you live there, you may have only five hundred monks."

FŪGAI: How do you know?

"That monastery is going to have more than one thousand monks."

FŪGAI: Is that all?

"Can you not find someone suitable among my monks?"

FŪGAI: Where is your eye to select a monk?

Ssu-ma T'ou-t'o continued, "I think Kuei-shan, the cook monk, will be the man."

FŪGAI: Nonsense!

Pai-chang then called Kuei-shan to tell him he must go to establish the new monastery.

FŪGAI: Better go easy!

The chief monk happened to hear the conversation and dashed to his teacher saying, "No one can say the cook monk is better than the chief monk."

FŪGAI: You do not know yourself.

Pai-chang then called the monks together, told them the situation, and said that anyone who gave a correct answer to his question would be a candidate.

FŪGAI: Upright judge!

Pai-chang then pointed to a water pitcher standing on the floor and asked, "Without using its name, tell me what it is."

FŪGAI: I can see the teacher's glaring eyes.

The chief monk said, "You cannot call it a wooden shoe."

FŪGAI: Some chief monk!

When no one else answered, Pai-chang turned to Kuei-shan. Kuei-shan stepped forward, tipped over the pitcher with his foot, then left the room.

FŪGAI: Nothing new.

Pai-chang smiled, "The chief monk lost."

FŪGAI: Upright judge!

Kuei-shan was made head of the new monastery, where he lived many years teaching more than one thousand monks in Zen.

FŪGAI: Not only one thousand monks, but all the Buddhas, past, present, and future, and all the Bodhisattvas from the ten quarters.

GENRŌ: Fortunately, Pai-chang put up a pitcher as a stake so the monk could tip it over. Suppose I point to the Southern Mountain and say, "Do not call it the Southern Mountain, then what do you call it?" If you say you cannot call it a wooden shoe, you are no better than the chief monk. You cannot tip it over as Kuei-shan did. Now, what do you do? Anyone among you who has real Zen transcending these opinions, answer me.

FŪGAI: I will kick the teacher.

NYOGEN: Even though all the monks were stupid none would say, "Wooden shoe," when pointing to the Southern Mountain. When Fūgai said, "I will kick the teacher," he probably meant both Pai-chang and Genrō. If I were Genrō, I would point to the bamboo broom outside the window and ask the monks to name it without saying its name. You cannot call it a dustpan nor can you kick out the broom. If I were Fūgai, I would take the broom and sweep the ground.

GENRŌ:

Just pick up the pitcher and measure short or long,

> [FŪGAI: What are you going to do with it? It has no measure; how can you name it short or long?]

Thus, transcending measurement, expose the entire contents.

> [That's what I say!]

See what one foot can do!

> [Precious, incomparable foot!]

One kick and the monastery is established on Kuei-shan.

> [That foot should grind emptiness to dust.]

75. A Monk in Meditation

The librarian saw a monk sitting in meditation in his library a
long time.

FŪGAI: Is he not a monk?

The librarian asked, "Why do you not read the sutras?"

FŪGAI: I would like to say to the monk, "Are you not sitting
in the wrong place?" Also I would like to ask the librarian
what kind of sutra he means.

The monk answered, "I do not know how to read."

FŪGAI: A lovable illiterate!

"Why do you not ask someone who knows?" suggested the librarian.

FŪGAI: Here you have slipped.

The monk stood up, asking politely, "What is this?"

FŪGAI: Poison oak!

The librarian remained silent.

FŪGAI: Good imitation.

GENRŌ: The monk stood and the librarian remained silent. Are
not these well-written sutras?

No special light is needed to read this sutra.

[FŪGAI: Fortunately, there is enough light to illumine
the darkness.]

Each character is clearly illumined.

[It cannot be translated.]

Standing without touching a book,

[Why hold what you already have?]

Five thousand sutras are read in a flash.

[What of the sutra no one can read? My teacher was
tardy with this comment.]

76. Ti-ts'ang's Peony

Ti-ts'ang took a trip with his two elder monks, Chang-ch'ing and
Pao-fu, to see the famous painting of a peony on a screen.

FŪGAI: Monks, you should wipe the film from your eyes.

Pao-fu said, "Beautiful peony!"

FŪGAI: Do not allow your eyes to cheat you.

Chang-ch'ing said, "Do not trust your visual organs too much."

FŪGAI: I say, "Do not trust your auditory organs."

Ti-ts'ang said, "It is too bad. The picture is already spoiled."

FŪGAI: The mouth is the cause of all trouble.

NYOGEN: Monks have no business going to see pictures, but once they see them, they must penetrate the canvas. Years ago a Sōtō Zen master went to Chicago, where he was invited by a friend to go through a slaughter house. He fainted before he had completed the inspection. He told me of the incident when he returned to San Francisco, and I told him monks should not go to such places, but once in, they must see thoroughly. My remark did not please him very much because he considered himself very kindhearted, and as abbot of a great Japanese temple, he did not appreciate these words from a nameless monk in America.

GENRŌ: Pao-fu enjoyed seeing the beautiful picture. Chang-ch'ing lost the opportunity of enjoying it himself because he was minding another's business. When Ti-ts'ang said, "It is too bad, the picture is already spoiled," is he joining Pao-fu or condemning Chang-ch'ing?

Chao-ch'ang skilfully painted the king of flowers.

[FŪGAI: The picture needs polishing.]

Colorful brocade opens to reveal perfume within.

[A pungent fragrance is unpleasant.]

Bees and butterflies encircle the bloom with pleasure.

[Mankind also has insects attracted by flowers.]

Do the three monks discuss the real or the painted flower?

[See the sign, DO NOT TOUCH!]

77. Tung-shan's Advice

Tung-shan said to his monks, "You monks should know there is an even higher knowledge in Buddhism."

FŪGAI: When one tries to know the higher, he falls lower.

A monk stepped forward and asked, "What is the higher Buddhism?"

FŪGAI: That monk was cheated by Buddha and the patriarchs.

Tung-shan answered, "It is not Buddha."

FŪGAI: Selling horsemeat labeled prime beef!

NYOGEN: A Zen monk tries hard to attain something superior to ordinary Buddhist knowledge. He is like a horse galloping to reach a handful of hay suspended in front of his nose from a pole attached to his halter. The only way is for the horse to stop running, allow the pole to slip from his back, and eat the hay. Tung-shan merely wished to encourage beginners in aiming for attainment, but when he was asked about the superior knowledge, he must answer, "It is not Buddha." Here Buddha stands for enlightenment and not for the person who attained enlightenment in India twenty-five centuries ago.

GENRŌ: Tung-shan is so kind. He is like a fond grandparent who forgets his dignity to play with the children and is heedless of the ridicule of spectators. Followers of his teaching must remember this and repay his kindness with gratitude.

FŪGAI: When one tries to repay, he himself makes heavy debts.

NYOGEN: Tung-shan was one of the founders of the Sōtō school. After Fūgai there was no greater teacher. The Rinzai school might scorn Tung-shan's answer in the belief that the monk deserved a blow. It is like the coldness of winter compared to the spring breeze. Americans may take either school, according to their choice.

GENRŌ:

Tung-shan's Zen is decorated with virtue and meditation,
[FŪGAI: It is worthless.]
Aimlessly misleading the people.

> [He is getting too old.]
> *The shadow of the bow in the glass,*
> [Lucky to know it is a shadow.]
> *Poisons the one who drinks the wine.*
> [One should be ashamed of himself.]

78. Yün-chü Sends Underclothing

Yün-chü, the master of a big monastery, sent underclothing to a monk living alone in a hut near the temple. He had heard that this monk sat long hours in meditation with no covering for his legs.

> FŪGAI: A benefit for a skinny person. That underclothing must have been inherited from Bodhidharma.
>
> NYOGEN: A prosperous monastery is called "fat," and a poor one "skinny." This idea is materialistic and lacks Zen spirit. When I first became a monk, I decided not to live in a "fat" temple but in a little hut like the monk of this story.

The monk refused the gift, saying, "I was born with my own underclothes."

> FŪGAI: Good monk! If you have it, I will give it to you. If you do not have it, I will take it from you.

Yün-chü sent a message asking, "What did you wear before you were born?"

> FŪGAI: Yün-chü is sending new clothes.

The monk could not answer.

> FŪGAI: Where are your two legs?

Later the monk died. At cremation sarira were found in the ashes and were brought to Yün-chü, who said, "Even had he left eighty-four bushels of sarira, they would not be worth the answer he failed to give me."

> FŪGAI: Government orders have no sentiment. No one can cheat a real master.
>
> GENRŌ: I will answer Yün-chü for the monk, "I could show you that, but it is so large you probably have no place to put it."
>
> FŪGAI: Good words, but not likely to be the monk's idea.
>
> NYOGEN: Some Japanese Zen students think the meditating

monk was cornered by Yün-chü's words and so kept quiet. What is wrong with this silence? I believe it an adequate answer. To begin with, he was not complaining. He was satisfied, and the sympathy expressed by the monastery was putting feet on the snake. Sarira, the sparkling gems said to be found in cremation ashes, are only products of Chinese legendary superstition. Yün-chü did not actually see them, but only gave lip service to the rumor. He is a poor story-eater. A good cremation will yield only ashes—monks, kings, or great masters.

GENRŌ:

> *Eighty-four bushels of sarira*
>> [FŪGAI: Bad odor!]
> *Cannot surpass one word that covers the universe.*
>> [The western family sends condolences to the eastern house.]
> *The mother's clothing—what a pity!*
>> [You are ungrateful to your mother.]
> *It cannot cover the present unsightliness.*
>> [Son of a millionaire stark naked.]

79. Tê-shan's Ultimate Teaching

Hsüeh-fêng asked Tê-shan, "Can I also share the ultimate teaching the old patriarchs attained?"

FŪGAI: He still has a tendency of kleptomania.

Tê-shan hit him with a stick, saying, "What are you talking about?"

FŪGAI: He is a kind old grandmother!

Hsüeh-fêng did not realize Tê-shan's meaning, so the next day he repeated his question.

FŪGAI: Is not one head enough?

Tê-shan answered, "Zen has no words, neither does it have anything to give."

FŪGAI: Poor statement.

笑見遊蜂飛蝶輩
信疑交抱障兒傍

"Bees and butterflies encircle the bloom with pleasure. Do the three monks discuss the real or the painted flower?"
　　—From Genrō's poem on Kōan 76, page 117

Yen-t'ou heard about the dialogue and said, "Tê-shan has an iron back-
bone, but he spoils Zen with his soft words."

> FŪGAI: One plays the flute and the other dances.
>
> NYOGEN: Yen-t'ou was a senior student under Tê-shan at the time Hsüeh-fêng was studying at the monastery. Fūgai is as bad an intruder as Yen-t'ou.
>
> GENRŌ: Tê-shan stole the sheep and Yen-t'ou proved it. Such a father! Such a son! A good combination.
>
> NYOGEN: A noble once told Confucius about an honest subject who proved in court that his father had stolen a sheep. Genrō took his comment from *The Analects*. A law-abiding person should stand for the law without regard for human sentiment. At least Zen must be carried without a shadow of sentiment. A good teacher will never spare a good student.
>
> GENRŌ:
>
> *Dragon head and snake tail!*
> [FŪGAI: What a monster!]
> *A toy stops a child's crying.*
> [Valuable toy.]
> *Yen-t'ou spoke as a bystander,*
> [A bystander can see.]
> *All for the allegiance to Dharma.*
> [Only a tithe was paid.]

80. *Pa-chiao Does Not Teach*

A monk asked Pa-chiao, "If there is a person who does not avoid
birth and death and does not realize Nirvana, do you teach such a person?"

> FŪGAI: What are you talking about?

Pa-chiao answered, "I do not teach him."

> FŪGAI: A good teacher does not waste words.

The monk said, "Why do you not teach him?"

> FŪGAI: What are you talking about?

"This old monk knows good and bad," Pa-chiao replied.

FŪGAI: The old fellow lost his tongue.

This dialogue between Pa-chiao and the monk was reported in other monasteries, and one day T'ien-t'ung said, "Pa-chiao may know good and bad, but he cannot take away a farmer's ox or a hungry man's food. If that monk asked me such a question, before he finished his sentence, I would hit him. Why? Because from the beginning I do not care about good and bad."

FŪGAI: The pot calls the kettle black.

NYOGEN: Pa-chiao was a Zen master of China by the name of Chi-ch'ê. The monk had postulated a free man without delusion or enlightenment, and wanted to know whether there was a higher teaching to enlighten such a person. Fūgai saw the nonsense of this hypothesis and warned the monk. Pa-chiao said, "I do not teach him," using the monk's own term "teach" without wasting his own words. When the monk could not understand this and asked why he did not teach, Pa-chiao's reply indicated he could recognize a person who needed teaching and one who did not. Fūgai's answer on Pa-chiao's having lost his tongue is in praise of this innocent answer.

The T'ien-t'ung mentioned here was a poet, who based his poems on the *Ts'ung-yung-lu,* or *Book of Equanimity.* His true name was Hung-chih. His reference to the ox and the food is the most rapid means of stripping delusions from the students, and that is why he would have struck the monk without discussing good and bad. Fūgai's slanderous comment is really in praise of Pa-chiao and T'ien-t'ung.

GENRŌ: Pa-chiao still uses the gradual method, whereas T'ien-t'ung employs the lightning flash. T'ien-t'ung's method can be easily understood, but few will see Pa-chiao's work clearly.

FŪGAI: What shall I say about your work?

GENRŌ:

There are many different drugs to cure an illness.

[FŪGAI: Thieves in peace time!]

Arrest a person without using handcuffs.
    [A hero in war time!]
Warcraft and medicine must be studied thoroughly.
    [Paradise does not need such art.]
Orchid in spring, chrysanthemum in autumn.
    [Excessively beautiful flowers cause congestion in the
    park.]

81. Kao-t'ing Strikes a Monk

A monk came from Chia-shan and bowed to Kao-t'ing.

FŪGAI: What are you doing!

Kao-t'ing immediately struck the monk.

FŪGAI: The kōan is vivid here.

*The monk said, "I came especially to you and paid homage with a bow.
Why do you strike me?"*

FŪGAI: What are you saying? Why do you not bow again?

Kao-t'ing struck the monk again and drove him from the monastery.

FŪGAI: Pure gold has a golden sheen.

The monk returned to Chia-shan, his teacher, and related the incident.

FŪGAI: It is a good thing you have someone to talk with.

"Do you understand or not?" asked Chia-shan.

FŪGAI: What can you do with a dead snake?

"No, I do not understand it," answered the monk.

FŪGAI: Good words, but not from you.

*"Fortunately, you do not understand," Chia-shan continued. "If you
did, I would be dumbfounded."*

FŪGAI: Good contrast to Kao-t'ing's action.

NYOGEN: Genrō adds his usual comment, but this one is not
    worth translating.

GENRŌ:
    The monk bows and Kao-t'ing strikes;
        [FŪGAI: What would you do if the monk had not
        bowed and you had not struck?]
    New etiquette for the monastery.

[Independent of convention.]

Not only is Chia-shan's mouth closed,

[Double indemnity.]

The wheel of Dharma is smashed.

[Expresses gratitude.]

NYOGEN: American Zen is running sideways writing books, lecturing, referring to theology, psychology, and what not. Someone should stand up and smash the whole thing to pieces, then true Dharma would be maintained in this land of liberty and righteousness.

82. Yen-t'ou's Ax

Tê-shan, Yen-t'ou's teacher, once told him, "I have two monks in this monastery who have been with me for many years. Go and examine them."

FŪGAI: Why do you not go yourself?

Yen-t'ou carried an ax to the little hut where the two monks were meditating.

FŪGAI: Have you wiped your eyes well?

Yen-t'ou raised the ax, saying, "If you say a word of Zen, I will cut off your heads. If you do not say anything, I will also decapitate you."

FŪGAI: Waves without wind.

The two monks continued their meditation, completely ignoring Yen-t'ou.

FŪGAI: Stone Buddhas.

Yen-t'ou threw down the ax, saying, "You are true Zen students."

FŪGAI: He is buying and selling himself.

He then returned to Tê-shan and related the incident.

FŪGAI: A defeated general had better not discuss warfare.

"I see your side well," Tê-shan agreed, "but, tell me, how is the other side?"

FŪGAI: Who are the others?

"Tung-shan may admit them," replied Yen-t'ou, "but they should not be admitted under Tê-shan."

FŪGAI: Should one go to the country of mosquitoes because he dislikes the country of fleas?

NYOGEN: Tung-shan would meditate with his monks, seldom using kōans, but Tê-shan would try to corner them with a threat. I join Fūgai in asking, "Have you wiped your eyes well?" Just because Zen is divided into two major schools does not mean that either school should never employ the other's methods.

GENRŌ: Why did Yen-t'ou say the two monks should be in Tung-shan's school but were not suitable for Tê-shan's? Real readers of the *Tetteki Tōsui* should meditate on this answer.

FŪGAI: Why did Genrō make this remark that readers should meditate?

GENRŌ:

Two iron bars barricade the entrance,
> [FŪGAI: How can you open them?]

One arrow passes between them.
> [That arrow is not strong enough.]

It is not necessary to discuss Tê-shan's method;
> [Very hard to glimpse it.]

After all, Tê-shan surrendered.
> [Sometimes a pet dog will bite.]

NYOGEN: Instead of sending Yen-t'ou, Tê-shan should have been pleased with the two monks. Yen-t'ou always made trouble. In my opinion Tê-shan is defeated, but not Yen-t'ou. When I have a visitor who likes to argue, I serve him tea, not allowing him to talk much while we are sipping, and he must leave after the third cup.

83. Yang-shan Draws a Line

Kuei-shan said to his disciple, Yang-shan, "All day you and I were talking Zen...

> FŪGAI: Both of you have tongues?

What did we accomplish after all?"

> FŪGAI: Formless words.

Yang-shan drew a line in the air with his finger.

FŪGAI: Why do you take such trouble?

Kuei-shan continued, "It was a good thing you dealt with me. You might cheat anyone else."

FŪGAI: The teacher lost the game.

GENRŌ: There are hundreds and thousands of Samadhis and countless principles of Buddhism, but all of them are included in Yang-shan's line. If anyone wishes to know something beyond those Samadhis or to sift out the best principles, look here at what I am doing.

FŪGAI: Bad imitator!

GENRŌ:

The miracles of these two monks surpass Moggallana's.
    [FŪGAI: Both are hallucinations.]
All day long the sham battle rages.
    [A battlefield on a pinpoint.]
What do they accomplish after all?
    [No words, no thought.]
One finger pokes the hole in emptiness.
    [Most awkward. When the clouds are gone, the sky is limitless.]

NYOGEN: Kuei-shan was taking a nap one day when Yang-shan came and greeted him. Kuei-shan turned sleepily to the wall. Yang-shan asked, "Why did you do that?" "I just had a dream," Kuei-shan replied, "can you interpret it for me?" Yang-shan left the room, returning a few moments later with a basin of cold water for his teacher's face. Soon Hsiang-yen also came to greet his teacher, whereat Kuei-shan said, "Your brother monk has just interpreted my dream. What is your interpretation?" Hsiang-yen went out quietly and returned with a cup of tea for his teacher. Kuei-shan commented, "You two monks perform miracles like Moggallana's." Moggallana is supposed to have performed miracles, but I must congratulate Buddha Sakyamuni for having such good disciples in China almost two thousand years after his death.

84. Ch'ien-fêng's One Road

A monk asked Ch'ien-fêng, "The one road of Nirvana leads into the ten quarters of Buddhaland. Where does it begin?" Ch'ien-fêng raised his walking stick to draw a horizontal line in the air, "Here."

FŪGAI: A white cloud obscures the road.

This monk later asked Yün-mên the same question.

FŪGAI: Are you lost again?

Yün-mên held up his fan and said, "This fan jumps up to the thirty-third heaven and hits the presiding deity on the nose, then comes down to the Eastern Sea and hits the holy carp. The carp becomes a dragon, which brings a flood of rain."

FŪGAI: A chatterbox makes a storm in the blue sky.

NYOGEN: Ch'ien-fêng shows the road of Zen, whereas Yün-mên exaggerates its action. Chinese people sometimes have had a tendency to exaggerate. The sphere of the microscope also shows the Buddhaland. Why not begin with the road of the amoeba? If I were asked a foolish question like this, I would say, "Watch your step."

GENRŌ: Ch'ien-fêng's answer provokes innocent people in vain; Yün-mên rattles around like a dry pea in a box. If anyone asked me this question, I would say, "Can't you see, you blind fool?"

FŪGAI: I would say to the monk, "I respect you for coming such a distance."

GENRŌ:

A hundred flowers follow the first bloom;
    [FŪGAI: For whom?]
They will festoon each field and garden.
    [Let's have a picnic.]
The eastern breeze blows gently everywhere;
    [Don't forget the seasonless season.]
Each branch has the perfect color of spring.
    [Beautiful picture of fairyland.]

85. Hsüan-sha's Iron Boat

When Hsüan-sha was studying Zen under Hsüeh-fêng, a brother monk named Kuang said, "If you can attain something in Zen, I will make an iron boat and sail the high seas."

FŪGAI: A logical statement.

Many years later Hsüan-sha became a Zen master, with Kuang studying under him as an attendant monk. One day Hsüan-sha said, "Have you built your iron boat?"

FŪGAI: Are you trying to sink that boat?

Kuang remained silent.

FŪGAI: The boat floats all right.

NYOGEN: Hsüan-sha was ordained as a monk when he was thirty years old. Before then he had been a simple fisherman. Some of the monks scornfully called him, "Impossible One." Kuang's comment was in this tone because at that time a metal ship epitomized the impossible. His remark probably encouraged Hsüan-sha in meditation, so Hsüan-sha is indebted to Kuang in that respect. When Hsüan-sha had fulfilled his study, Kuang entered his monastery and served him. I admire Kuang's modesty and perseverance and do not believe Hsüan-sha asked his question in retaliation, but used the words as a synonym of attainment. It was only intimate family conversation.

GENRŌ: If I were Kuang, I would say, "Have you attained your Zen?"

FŪGAI: Ha! Ha!

GENRŌ:

An iron boat froze on the sea.
　　　[FŪGAI: I would not like to sail that boat.]
The kōan from the past is fulfilled.
　　　[Do not mention the past; live in the present.]
Do not say Kuang kept silent;
　　　[What can he do?]

"Orchid in spring, chrysanthemum in autumn."
—From Genrō's poem on Kōan 80, page 125

Uncle Hsüan-sha, have you attained?
> [Ta-hui said, "After eighteen attainments, all attainments flourish.]

86. *Yang-shan Sits in Meditation*

When Yang-shan was sitting in meditation, a monk came quietly and stood by him.
> FŪGAI: Such a trick won't work.

Yang-shan recognized the monk, so he drew a circle in the dust with the ideograph for water beneath it, then looked at the monk.
> FŪGAI: What kind of charm is it?

The monk could not answer.
> FŪGAI: A sprinter falls down.

> NYOGEN: Yang-shan's attitude was like that of a spectator on the beach watching quietly as the waves curl and wet his feet. If I were the monk, I would make myself Yang-shan, raise my robe above the water and step out, or push Yang-shan from his meditation seat saying, "Waves! Waves!"

> GENRŌ: This monk committed petty larceny and could not even escape after his deed. Yang-shan was ready at any time to light the candle. Alas! The opportunity is gone.

> GENRŌ:

Letter water cannot quench thirst;
> [FŪGAI: But I see the giant billows rising.]

Nor pictured rice-cakes feed hunger.
> [Here is a trayful of cakes.]

Yang-shan's action brought no merit.
> [That is true Zen.]

Why does he not give the monk the big stick?
> [It will be too late. The big stick is already broken.]

87. *Ch'an-yüeh Snaps His Fingers*

Ch'an-yüeh, the monk poet, wrote a poem containing the following two verses:

When Zen students meet, they may snap their fingers at each other.

FŪGAI: Do not overlook it.

But how few know what it means.

FŪGAI: Do you know, it is the sword that cuts the tongue.

Ta-sui heard of this poem and, meeting Ch'an-yüeh, he asked, "What is the meaning?"

FŪGAI: When the rabbit appears the hawk is off after him.

Ch'an-yüeh did not answer.

FŪGAI: Did I not say before, he does not know!

NYOGEN: Ch'an-yüeh wrote many good poems, which proved his attainment, but these verses seem to have been taken from their context. Ta-sui approached the poet beyond the verse, and Ch'an-yüeh faltered. Like editors of a slanderous yellow paper seeking only their own benefit, Genrō and Fūgai took up the anecdote as a kōan at the expense of Ch'an-yüeh's reputation.

GENRŌ: If I were Ch'an-yüeh, I would snap my fingers at Ta-sui.

FŪGAI: So far it is good, but instead, no one can understand it.

GENRŌ:

One snap of the fingers cannot be easily criticized,

[FŪGAI: Cut the finger off.]

But he must not snap them until he has passed 110 castles.

[Do you want to wait for Maitreya?]

I should ask the crippled old woman who sells sandals,

[She cannot understand the feeling of other feet.]

"Why do you not walk to the capital barefoot?"

[It is difficult to wash one's own back.]

NYOGEN: It is recorded in the Avatamsaka Sutra that Suddhana passed one hundred and ten castles searching for teachers, meeting many people to whom he paid homage, until at last he reached the gate of Maitreya. He snapped his fingers, the gate opened, and there he met Samantabhadra, who ended his journey. There is a Chinese proverb, "The crippled old woman always speaks of the comfort of the grass sandals she sells." Fūgai was quick enough to mention the difficulty of washing one's own back, but what would he say to my device from Woolworth's for this purpose?

88. Yüeh-shan's Lake

Yüeh-shan asked a newly-arrived monk, "Where have you come from?"

FŪGAI: Are you enjoying the atmosphere?

The monk answered, "From the Southern Lake."

FŪGAI: You give a glimpse of the lake view.

"Is the lake full or not?" inquired Yüeh-shan.

FŪGAI: Are you still interested in the lake?

"Not yet," the monk replied.

FŪGAI: He glanced at the lake.

"There has been so much rain, why isn't the lake filled?" Yüeh-shan asked.

FŪGAI: Yüeh-shan invited the monk to see the lake, actually.

The monk remained silent.

FŪGAI: He must have drowned.

NYOGEN: Zen monks like to dwell intimately with nature. Most Chinese monasteries were built in the mountains or by a lake. Zen records many dialogues between teacher and monks concerning natural beauty, but there must also be many monks who never asked questions, simply allowing themselves to merge with nature. They are the real supporters of Zen—better than the chatterboxes with all their noise in an empty box.

GENRŌ: If I were the monk, I would say to Yüeh-shan, "I will wait until you have repaired the bottom."

FŪGAI: It was fortunate the monk remained silent.

NYOGEN: Genrō sometimes sounds like a shyster with unnecessary argument.

GENRŌ:

> *The thread of Karma runs through all things;*
>   [FŪGAI: One can pick up anything as a kōan.]
> *Recognition makes it a barricade.*
>   [If you look behind there is no barricade.]
> *The poor monk asked about a lake,*
>   [Go on! Jump in and swim!]
> *Made an imaginary road to heaven.*
>   [Where are you standing?]

89. *Hsüeh-fêng's Wooden Ball*

One day Hsüeh-fêng began a lecture to the monks gathered around the little platform by rolling down a wooden ball.

FŪGAI: A curved cucumber.

Hsüan-sha went after the ball, picked it up and replaced it on the stand.

FŪGAI: A round melon.

NYOGEN: When Yüan-wu gave a lecture on Hsüeh-tou's selected kōans and poems, he criticized one phrase after another, then published them all in book form under the title, *Pi-yen-chi*, or *Blue Rock Collection*. After his death, his disciple, Ta-hui, gathered all the publications together in front of the temple and made a bonfire of them. What the teacher builds in shape must be destroyed by the disciples in order to keep the teachings from becoming an empty shell. Western philosophers create their own theory, then followers continue to repair the outer structure until it no longer resembles the original. In Zen we say, "Kill Buddha and the patriarchs; only then can you give them eternal life."

GENRŌ: Hsüeh-fêng began but did not end; Hsüan-sha ended but did not begin. Both are incomplete. Now, tell me, monks, which way is better?

NYOGEN: Neither of them.

FŪGAI: When water runs through the bamboo forest, its color is green. When wind blows across the flowers, each breath is fragrant.

GENRŌ:

Hold it or let it go.

[FŪGAI: No more, no less.]

Teacher and disciple contradict each other.

[Real congeniality.]

Zen students of the world,

[A real student never studies.]

Do not make this kōan a model.

[Beautiful example.]

90. The Broken Tray

There was once a little hut called, Fei-t'ien, meaning "rich field,"
where a monk lived for thirty years.

FŪGAI: Maybe he did not know how to move.

He had only one tray made of clay.

FŪGAI: Expensive things are not always precious.

One day a monk, who studied under him, broke that tray accidentally.

FŪGAI: The real treasure appears from the breaking.

Each day the teacher asked the student to replace it.

FŪGAI: Why do you want another?

Each time the disciple brought a new one, the teacher threw it out saying,
"This is not it. Give me back my old one."

FŪGAI: I would open my hands and laugh.

NYOGEN: No one knows the name of this monk, but his statement, "This is not it. Give me back my old one," was worth recording.

GENRŌ: If I were the disciple, I would say, "Wait until the sun rises in the west."

FŪGAI: I will search for it before I am born.

GENRŌ:

> *It is broken;*
>> [FŪGAI: The whole tray remains.]
>
> *Run fast after it.*
>> [The sword disappears in the water.]
>
> *The disciple cannot understand it.*
>> [It has returned to him already.]
>
> *Call an iron kettle a bell.*
>> [You can call the earth heaven . . . what's wrong?]

91. *Fa-yen's Drop of Water*

*A monk asked Fa-yen, "What is a drop of water from the source
in the valley of the sixth patriarch?"*

FŪGAI: Squirt ink from your mouth into someone's face.

*Fa-yen said, "That is a drop of water from the source in the valley of the
sixth patriarch."*

FŪGAI: He uses poison as an antidote.

GENRŌ: Fa-yen never discounts from the fixed price.

FŪGAI: There is no fixed price.

GENRŌ:

> *This drop of water from the source;*
>> [FŪGAI: The Yellow River is polluted at the source.]
>
> *There is no worse poison. . . .*
>> [Whoever drinks, dies!]
>
> *Do not say you know warm or cold.*
>> [Who knows the taste?]
>
> *How many can drink it?*
>> [I have drunk it already.]

92. *Ts'ao-shan's Four "Don'ts"*

Ts'ao-shan said, "Do not follow the bird's road of mind."

FŪGAI: Do you prefer nomads?

NYOGEN: Did you ever hear of Kontiki?

"Do not clothe yourself before you are born."
>FŪGAI: Does nakedness bring happiness?
>
>NYOGEN: Tokuyae, the dancer, wears heavy clothing while dancing, and her grace flows into the cloth.

"Do not say the present minute is eternal."
>FŪGAI: Just show your face.
>
>NYOGEN: I do not like that face.

"Do not express yourself before birth."
>FŪGAI: Men should read without letters.
>
>NYOGEN: I understand ten thousand Chinese characters, but they do not bother me.
>
>GENRŌ: According to Ts'ao-shan's words I will ask you monks:
>>[FŪGAI: Go ahead! I will answer each one.]
>
>"First, you can go wherever you want, but what is the bird's road?"
>>[East or west?]
>
>"Second, you can wear any wardrobe now, but what did you wear before you were born?"
>>[No civilized person walks the street naked.]
>
>"Third, say whatever you like, but what is the present?"
>>[NYOGEN: Fūgai's comment is worthless to translate. I will say for him, "The question is too good to be answered."]
>
>"Fourth, you can express what you wish, but where were you before you were born?"
>>[FŪGAI: The conjuror knows the trick.]
>
>GENRŌ:
>
>*Ts'ao-shan's home remedy is peppery;*
>>[FŪGAI: It is more soothing than honey.]
>
>*The purpose is to kill the people.*
>>[When all are killed there arises the living man.]
>
>*The three-foot sword glitters;*
>>[Buddha and the patriarchs will be scared to death.]
>
>*Each cut makes the sword sharper.*
>>[Do not cut yourself!]

93. Tê-shan's Lion

As Tê-shan was working in the garden one day, he saw a monk approaching up the road. Tê-shan closed the gate.

FŪGAI: Interview finished.

The monk knocked on the gate.

FŪGAI: Delayed action.

Tê-shan said, "Who is it?"

FŪGAI: A monster!

The monk answered, "A lion cub."

FŪGAI: The lion cub enters the fox's lair.

Tê-shan opened the gate.

FŪGAI: He puts his head in the lion's mouth.

The monk made a bow to the teacher.

FŪGAI: His fur does not look like a lion's.

Tê-shan jumped on his back as he would on a small lion, held him down, and said, "You devil! Where have you been?"

FŪGAI: That is the way to raise a cub.

GENRŌ: At first I thought he was a real cub, but now I see his strength is less than a fox. He should have jumped Tê-shan the moment the gate was opened, holding him helpless.

FŪGAI: You devil.

NYOGEN: Kangetsu said it was a good show. The curtain should be lowered to mark the conclusion. I agree with her. Genrō, like a country bumpkin, made a noise for nothing. The midsummer breeze enters the room where we, Kangetsu and I, work together. Why should we question the breeze? What is it? Where is it from? Just welcome it, calling it neither devil nor angel.

GENRŌ:

He calls himself a lion, and visits a lion tamer.

　　[FŪGAI: Roaring like a lion.]

That voice shatters the monastery.

　　[The echo returns from mountain and valley.]

十分春色
顯枝枝

" Each branch has the perfect color of spring."
—From Genrō's poem on Kōan 84, page 129

The lion became a donkey,
> [He should learn tumbling.]
Defeated before he could kick.
> [No rain after thunder.]

94. Living Alone

A monk came to Yün-chü and asked, "How can I live alone at the top of the mountain?"

FŪGAI: You are lost in a cloud.

Yün-chü answered, "Why do you give up your Zen-dō in the valley and climb the mountain?"

FŪGAI: This is not the way to handle ghosts.

NYOGEN: American friends often ask me how to find the "quiet place to meditate." My usual answer is, "Can you not find a quiet spot in your home?" No matter how busy one's daily life is, he can find certain minutes in which to meditate and a certain place to sit quietly. Merely pining for a quiet place away from his own home is entirely wrong. This monk could not harmonize himself with other monks in the Zen-dō and wished to live alone on a mountain peak. Even though Yün-chü cornered the monk with the question, no wonder Fūgai thought Yün-chü too luke warm in his method.

If I were Yün-chü, I would demand that the monk tell me where he is at this moment. If he hesitated, I would push him out of the room immediately.

GENRŌ: If I were Yün-chü, I would say to the monk, "If you do not neglect your own Zen-dō, I will allow you to stay on the mountain peak. But how can you stay on the mountain without neglecting your own Zen-dō?"

FŪGAI: Destroy that Zen-dō and that mountain!

NYOGEN: Fūgai is like an anarchist. I do not wish to associate with this radical monk. Genrō's first remark is splendid. Why did he add the last? Look at my associates! They are all good businessmen and housewives. None of them neglect their work to pursue Zen. Any teaching that is apart from daily life is not real teaching.

GENRŌ:

> *Yün-chü pushed the monk to the abyss,*
>> [FŪGAI: There is no higher or wider place.]
>
> *And threw him into it,*
>> [Gave him eternal life.]
>
> *Where he will remain for all eternity.*
>> [No entrance, no exit.]
>
> *His method is superior to other teachers'.*
>> [One should have gratitude.]

NYOGEN: Hey!

95. *Lin-chi's Real Eye*

Ma-ku asked Lin-chi, "Avalokiteçvara has one thousand hands and each hand has an eye, which is the real eye?"

FŪGAI: Which is not the real eye?

Lin-chi answered, "Avalokiteçvara has one thousand hands and each hand has an eye, which is the real eye? Now tell me! Quick!"

FŪGAI: The enemy is defeated with its own weapons.

Ma-ku pulled Lin-chi from his seat then sat in his place.

FŪGAI: A comet comes close to another constellation.

Lin-chi stood up and asked, "Why?"

FŪGAI: The whole army retreats by command.

KANGETSU: Ma-ku did not keep his aim steady.

Lin-chi shouted, "Katz!" and pulled Ma-ku from his seat in turn.

FŪGAI: Sleeping dragon.

NYOGEN: Hold the enemy's spear and attack him with it.

Ma-ku left the room quietly.

FŪGAI: Two generals understand each other.

NYOGEN: In Chinese history K'ung-ming, a well known general, was suddenly surrounded by the enemy under the command of Chung-t'a. K'ung-ming was alone at the time, his men away on leave. K'ung-ming stepped out on the balcony of a tower overlooking the enemy and played his harp. Chung-t'a knew of K'ung-ming's superior strategy and, afraid that K'ung-ming's men were hiding prepared for attack, suddenly ordered his own men to retreat. K'ung-ming is known as Master of the Sleeping Dragon, whom none could defeat. Fūgai's comment refers to this story.

Avalokiteçvara has one thousand eyes, but there is only one real eye. That real eye manifests itself as the one thousand eyes. It is like the moon reflected simultaneously in a thousand lakes. Does the lake invite the moon, or does the moon come down to the lake? Which is host and which is guest? Foxy Lin-chi purposely made the question, "Why?" before his "Katz!" Ma-ku should toss back the "Katz" and leave abruptly. Too bad the battle was lost so ingloriously.

GENRŌ: Lin-chi's question, "Why?" would make anyone hesitate. If one of you monks can answer him correctly, you can walk with your arms swinging freely at your side. This is the secret of Lin-chi's teaching.

FŪGAI: Don't shout it from the housetops!

GENRŌ:

I thought T'ien-tan was a good fighter.

　　[FŪGAI: A good commander is seldom found.]

His changeable strategy scared even demons.

　　[One thousand sages cannot follow the highest road.]

When he used the fire-carrying bulls to fight,

　　[One hundred battles, one hundred victories.]

He regained seventy castles at a time.

　　[From the beginning he did not lose.]

NYOGEN: T'ien-tan was another fighter in China. When he was short of soldiers, he utilized bulls to fight by lighting bundles of fire on their backs, thus winning a victory from the jaws of defeat.

Monks should not talk of war and fighting. It is against the precepts of Buddhism. There are many examples that could be used rather than these; even a branch of flowers would make a better illustration. In the future, around the year 2100, Zen students may forget what warfare was and enjoy their Zen in peaceful gardens filled with the spring breeze.

96. Yen-t'ou's Three Worlds

A monk asked Yen-t'ou, "When three worlds* threaten me, what shall I do?"

> FŪGAI: Carry them on your shoulder.

Yen-t'ou answered, "Sit down."

> FŪGAI: You have given him another burden.

"I do not understand," replied the monk.

> FŪGAI: You do not even know you have slipped.

Yen-t'ou said, "Pick up the other mountain and bring it to me, then I will tell you."

> FŪGAI: A man who makes himself a Buddha instantly should also make others Buddhas!
>
> GENRŌ: If Yen-t'ou had not given his second answer, his Zen would have been questioned by others.
>
> NYOGEN: One might think he meant to sit down on the three worlds, or to make the monk seat himself. Kangetsu-san, let us have tea.
>
> GENRŌ: If the monk asked me what to do when the three worlds threatened, I would answer, "World of delusion, world of material, and world of immaterial." If the monk then said he could not understand it, I would answer, "The eastern mountain stands on the river."
>
> FŪGAI: Let me carry on my kōan: If the monk questioned me, I should say, "A dew drop." If he still insisted he could not understand, I would say, "It turns to gems on a lotus leaf."

* "The three worlds" refers to the world of desire, the world of the immaterial, and the world of the material.

GENRŌ:

> *Three worlds piled up;*
>> [FŪGAI: Waves break on the heavens.]
>
> *The Zen monk sits on one cushion.*
>> [Throw that cushion out!]
>
> *Yen-tʻou opened his mouth to say,*
>> [The world is still in my ear.]
>
> *"Pick up that mountain and bring it to me."*
>> [Last night someone stole that mountain.]

97. Buddha's Body

When the Buddha was preaching the Nirvana Sutra,

> FŪGAI: Incomplete. Where were you before that? Have you not always been in the same place?
>
> NYOGEN: He has never been any place. If you think he has, you must admit a portion of India. Why don't you wait until he is finished?

he rubbed his chest with his hand, saying, "You should observe my golden body thoroughly, otherwise you will regret it later."

> NYOGEN: Buddha expected to enter Parinirvana, thus, this remark.
>
> FŪGAI: Shh! You fox, you have cheated many people and now you try to eliminate your mistake.
>
> NYOGEN: I told you to listen well.

"If you say, 'Buddha enters Parinirvana,' you are not my disciple."

> FŪGAI: I will say loudly, "Buddha enters Parinirvana! Buddha enters Parinirvana!"

"If you say, 'Buddha does not enter Parinirvana,' you are not my disciple."

> FŪGAI: I will say loudly, "Buddha does not enter Parinirvana! Buddha does not enter Parinirvana!"
>
> GENRŌ: Buddha died a thousand years ago. If you say he is still here, you are admitting he has not entered Nirvana. If you say he is not here, you are admitting he has entered Nirvana. If you say he has neither entered Parinirvana nor not entered

Parinirvana, then you must admit he was neither here nor not here. Then, where is his golden body? Each of you go to your own room and take a good rest.

FŪGAI: My teacher, you go to your room first.

GENRŌ:

Old teacher was too busy before he traveled.

[FŪGAI: Why don't you prepare before that?]

He showed the golden light;

[Who sees it is blind.]

He sealed his disciples' mouths.

[There has never been anything to say.]

Family scandal should be kept quiet.

[Plug your ears before you steal.]

98. Hsiu-ching Uses the Game

Hsiu-ching was the managing monk of Lê-p'u's monastery.

FŪGAI: A very responsible position.

One day he struck with his gavel and ordered, "Monks from the first to the middle seats, go out to work the fields. The remaining monks go to the mountain for wood."

FŪGAI: A general orders his soldiers.

"What is Manjusri to do?" asked the chief monk.

NYOGEN: Each Zen-dō has a statue or painting of either Manjusri or Bodhidharma.

FŪGAI: He is really the chief monk.

"My order goes only to those monks seated on cushions," answered the manager monk, "Manjusri has nothing to do with the order."

NYOGEN: In the Diamond Sutra we read: "Subhuti, if a man should declare that the Tathagata is the one who comes, or goes, or sits, or lies he does not understand the meaning of my teaching."

FŪGAI: He knows his position very well.

Later Yüan-wu commented on the dialogue, "Hsiu-ching made a won-

*derful performance. The chief monk's method was excellent to thread
nine spiral shells."*

FŪGAI: Nothing excellent to me.

NYOGEN: Some one asked Confucius how to thread nine
spiral shells, but he could not answer. A woman told him to
put honey at one end and let an ant carry the thread through.

*"This is all right, but to open interlocking rings, I have a different
method."*

FŪGAI: Let's see it.

NYOGEN: Another question in China was to solve the puzzle of
interlocking rings, which no wise man could do, but a woman
smashed them with a hammer.

*Yüan-wu continued, "If I were questioned that way by the chief monk, I
would answer, 'The path is like a mirror. It does not r ve itself, but
reflects all that comes.'"*

FŪGAI: Break that mirror.

GENRŌ: If anyone asked me—without threading nine spiral
shells or releasing interlocking rings—what Manjusri has to
do, I would hit him before he finished his question. Why?
Because those who cultivate the fields have only to do as
ordered, and those gathering wood also do as ordered.

NYOGEN: That is the actual order of Manjusri.

FŪGAI: Hsiu-ching shows Dharmakaya (Body of the law),
Yüan-wu speaks of Nirmanakaya (application), and Genrō
depicts Sambogakaya (results). If I were the manager monk,
I would hit the gavel and discharge the chief monk for
that day.

GENRŌ:

Threading nine spirals or crushing interlocking rings,
        [FŪGAI: Real wisdom works without thinking.]
The wheel of Dharma turns itself independently.
        [Great wisdom is like great stupidity.]
Confucius is wise, but he cannot defeat the woman.
        [Born, not made.]

The old pine tree grows on a snow-covered rock.
[It makes me shiver.]
*The early plum blossom anticipates the spring and smiles at the
fence.*
[I love that fragrance.]

99. Ta-tien's Age

Han-t'ui-chih asked Ta-tien, who had a monastery in the place
of exile, "How old are you?"*

FŪGAI: He is a different age from you.

Ta-tien held out his rosary and said, "Do you understand?"

FŪGAI: What trinkets are you using?

Han-t'ui-chih said, "No, I cannot understand."

FŪGAI: Don't you know what this rosary is?

*Ta-tien replied, "In the daytime there are one hundred eight beads, and
at night there are also one hundred eight."*

FŪGAI: Don't you know a better way to handle this student?

*Han-t'ui-chih was very much displeased because he could not understand
this old monk and returned home.*

FŪGAI: You are trying to hammer a nail in the sky.

At home his wife asked, "What makes you so displeased?"

FŪGAI: This is not a woman's problem.

The scholar then told his wife all that had happened.

FŪGAI: What is the good of it? Why do you argue your case as
though you protested to the emperor?

*"Why not go back to the monastery and ask the old monk what he
meant?" his wife suggested.*

FŪGAI: Fortunately, he has a better half.

*Next day, early in the morning, the Confucian scholar went to the
monastery, where he met the chief monk at the gate.*

---

* Han-t'ui-chih was a Confucian scholar with an appointment to the
Imperial Library, but was exiled eight thousand Chinese miles from the
capital because of his opposition to the emperor's worship of the Buddha's
ashes.

FŪGAI: Misfortune dogs his steps.

"Why are you here so early?" the chief monk asked.

FŪGAI: Why not?

"I wish to see your master and question him," Han-t'ui-chih answered.

FŪGAI: Do you know where he is?

"What is your business with him?" the chief monk asked, so the Confucian repeated his story.

FŪGAI: The master never said these words. You are slandering him.

"Why don't you ask me?" the chief monk inquired.

NYOGEN: Upstart!

Han-t'ui-chih then asked, "What does 'One hundred eight beads in the daytime and one hundred eight beads at night' mean?"

FŪGAI: Search the *I-ching*.

The chief monk clicked his teeth three times.

FŪGAI: You are inviting trouble.

At last Han-t'ui-chih met Ta-tien and once more asked his question, whereupon the master clicked his teeth three times.

FŪGAI: Do not think you are seeing Zen.

"I know," said the Confucian, "all Buddhism is alike."

FŪGAI: The moon is only one, but it illuminates the mountain and the valley differently.

"You do not say so," Ta-tien answered.

FŪGAI: Are you prepared to spill blood?

"Yes," said Han-t'ui-chih, "a few moments ago I met the chief monk at the gate and asked him the same question and he answered me in the same way."

FŪGAI: What are you saying? This same thing never happened before.

Ta-tien called the chief monk to him and said, "I understand you showed him Buddhism a few minutes ago. Is it true?"

FŪGAI: The battle lines are moving.

"Yes," answered the chief monk.

FŪGAI: This foolish one does not know how to turn himself out.

Ta-tien struck the chief monk and immediately expelled him from the monastery.

FŪGAI: When Wong commits murder, Wang will be hung.

GENRŌ: Why was the chief monk expelled? If it was punishment, the master himself did the same, why not punish himself? If he is not punished, why is he expelled? Here is the secret of Zen teaching, which has been and will be transmitted from generation to generation. If Ta-tien showed his Zen at that moment, he will not only spoil others, but will himself kill the life of wisdom. Do not be alarmed at the thunderstorm, monks, you will see countless stars in the sky later.

FŪGAI: After all, Ta-tien had a friend.

GENRŌ:

Day and night, one hundred eight. . . .
[FŪGAI: It ends and begins.]
What does it mean?
[It is clear seen face to face.]
Clicking the teeth brings expulsion.
[There was a good opportunity.]
Northern trees bear differently in the south.
[When the soil is changed that always happens.]
The doubts of the chief librarian increase;
[Your mirror is not well polished.]
Now he knows it is not so easy to handle Buddha's ashes.
[He thought it was imported, but it was made in China.]

100. Kuei-shan's Ten-Foot Square

Kuei-shan had a poem on the wall of his room:

Ten square feet of Kuei-shan,
[FŪGAI: When was it built?]
Too steep to climb
[I can walk as though it were flat.]

If anyone enters,
>   [Watch your step.]

He will become a great general.
>   [Do not forget there is another great general.]

Yün-fêng said of the poem, "Kuei-shan is a born Zen master."
>   FŪGAI: Apple sauce!

A monk asked Yün-fêng, "What poem are you going to write for your room?"
>   FŪGAI: Good question.

Yün-fêng replied by showing his poem:
>   FŪGAI: Imitator!

Ten square feet of Ts'ui-yen,
Never had a door.
>   [FŪGAI: Difficult to enter.]

Any monk who comes in,
>   [He is walking the edge of a sword.]

Immediately sees Ts'ui-yen.
>   [Skating on ice.]

The monk paid homage and stood up.
>   FŪGAI: What did he have to say?

Yün-fêng said, "Did you see Ts'ui-yen or not?"
>   FŪGAI: There is barbed wire all around.

The monk hesitated.
>   FŪGAI: I told you he could not enter.

Yün-fêng hit the monk's mouth with a mosquito brush.
>   FŪGAI: There! The door is open.

>   GENRŌ: Kuei-shan's room is hard to see but easy to enter.
>   Ts'ui-yen's room is easy to see but hard to enter. I also have
>   a poem in my room:

>   *That emptiness has neither in nor out.*
>   *If there is no in or out,*
>   *I ask you, monks,*
>   *How can you enter then?*

>   FŪGAI: I would not enter that room.

GENRŌ:

Even a steep cliff has toe holds;

[FŪGAI: There is a flat part on the steep;]

Flat ground hides a tiger trap.

[There is a steep place on the flat.]

Each established his monastery according to home routine.

[One has to do foolish actions to save others.]

Golden deeds gleam even now.

[Generation after generation carries troubles endlessly.]

NYOGEN SENZAKI passed from this world on the
5th of May, 1958. These were his last words:

> *"Friends in Dharma, be satisfied with your own heads.
> Do not put any false heads above your own. Then, minute
> after minute watch your steps closely. These are my last
> words to you."*

Nyogen Senzaki

Sōen Shaku on Nyogen Senzaki

IF THE hitting of Tê-shan's big stick covers me like rain, I will not be frightened. If the shouting of Lin-chi's "Katz," roars like a thunderstorm, I will not be surprised. If Punna's sermons are as fluent as running water and Sariputta's wisdom sparkles like the morning star, I will not envy them. If one keeps the precepts, consecrates his life, lives alone in a mountain hut, takes his meal once a day, fasts often, makes his body transparent with pure food, and performs Buddhist ceremonies six times a day, but lacks the vow to save all sentient beings, I cannot encourage myself to respect him.

My idea is shown in the Saddharma-pundarika Sutra as a character named "Bodhisattva Never-Despised." If in our day a Bodhisattva accomplishes realization of selflessness, using his hands only for loving-kindness as a mother cares for her baby, walks the road of life to serve him, rocks the cradle to comfort him, and thinks of all boys and girls as her own children, so a monk considers all workers on the different stages as his companions, makes a home without wife or children, gathers mentors with no discrimination of guest and host, speaks plain humanity, implying Buddha-nature, he will certainly bring my admiration and make me shed tears of sympathy. I wonder, how many monks or priests such as this are among the hundred thousand Buddhist workers in Japan?

Monk Nyogen tries to live the Bhikkhu's life according to the teaching of Buddha, to be non-sectarian with no connection to a temple or headquarters; therefore, he keeps no property of his own, refuses to hold a position in the priesthood, and conceals himself from noisy fame and glory. He has, however, the four vows—greater than worldly ambition, with Dharma treasures higher than any position, and loving-kindness more valuable than temple treasures. He walked out of my monastery and now wanders around the world, meeting young people, associating with their families, and making religion, education, ethics, and culture the steps to climb to the highest. He is still far from being a "Bodhisattva Never-Despised," but I consider him as a soldier of the crusade to restore the peaceful Buddha-land for all mankind and all sentient beings. Every step of continuation means success to him for this sort of endless work. I congratulate him this very moment.

Autumn 1901
Engaku Monastery
Kamakura

An Autobiographical Sketch

As Told to

One of His Students

YOU HAVE asked me about my past training and my work in America. I am merely a nameless and homeless monk. Even to think of my past embarrasses me. However, I have nothing to hide. But, you know, a monk renounces the world and wishes to attract as little attention as possible, so whatever you read here you must keep to yourself and forget about it.

My foster father began to teach me Chinese classics when I was five years old. He was a Kegon scholar, so he naturally gave me training in Buddhism. When I was eighteen years old, I had finished reading the Chinese Tripitaka, but now in this old age I do not remember what I read. Only his influence remains: to live up to the Buddhist ideals outside of name and fame and to avoid as far as possible the world of loss and gain. I studied Zen in the Sōtō school first, and in the Rinzai school later. I had a number of teachers from both schools, but I gained nothing. I love and respect Sōen Shaku more than all other teachers, but I do not feel like carrying all my teachers' names on my back like a sandwich man; it would almost defile them.

In those days one who passed all kōans called himself the first and best successor of his teacher and belittled others. My taste does not agree with this manner. It may be my foster father's influence, but I have never made any demarcation of my learning, so do not consider myself finished at any point. Even now I am not interested in inviting many friends to our meetings. You may laugh, but I am really a mushroom without a very deep root, no branches, no flowers, and probably no seeds.

After my arrival in this country in 1905, I simply worked through many stages of American life as a modern Sudhana—meditating alone in Golden Gate Park or studying hard in the public library of San Francisco. Whenever I could save money, I would hire a hall and give a talk on Buddhism, but this was not until 1922. I named our various meeting places a floating Zen-dō. At last in 1928 I established a Zen-dō, which I have carried with me as a snail his shell; thus, I came to Los Angeles in 1931. I feel only gratitude to my teachers and all my friends, and fold my hands palm to palm.

Nyogen Senzaki on His Zen-dō

BODHISATTVAS:

In the beginning this place was selected by some Japanese Buddhist friends as a shelter for Buddhist monks. My ideal as a Buddhist monk is to have no permanent place to stay, but to take a course of pilgrimage as a lone cloud floating freely in the blue sky. Even though I have been staying in this place two years and five months, I have always considered myself a pilgrim on a journey, making each day a transient stay. As it is a transient stay, I do not worry about tomorrow. It is to-day I am living with gratitude. What can my regret do with the happenings of yesterday? If I have to go away for a long trip, some other monk or monks may stay in this shelter, transiently, the same as I. As long as this principle of Anicca, the principle of impermanence, is practiced, this shelter will remain a Buddhist house. In fact, I am passing away every day. What you saw about me yesterday, you cannot see any more. Tomorrow you will meet a man who looks like Senzaki, thinks like Senzaki, and speaks like Senzaki, but he is not the Senzaki you met today. As long as you dwell in the understanding of Anatta, the principle of non-individuality, our relation will be Buddhistic.

If any of you have a desire to move our meditation hall to another location to increase your comfort and pleasure, you are clinging to delusions which are not Buddhistic at all. True Buddhists never proselytize. I did not ask you to come to this place; your own Buddha-nature guided you here. If a new location and a better house would attract more people, what would be the use of them if we had no Buddhist spirit within ourselves? Some may say they are satisfied with this location and house, but for the sake of strangers we must make it more attractive. This world is nothing but the phenomena of dissatisfaction. Wherever one goes, one must face some sort of suffering. This is the principle of Dukkha, the principle of suffering, which Buddha repeatedly stressed. Those who come for comfort and pleasure will never be satisfied in a Buddhist house. They have not belonged here from the beginning, so why should we try to attract them? This house is a shelter for Buddhist monks, and you, our honorable guests, should feel obliged to follow its principles. If you wish to meditate, I will join you in meditation. If you wish to study the scriptures, I will assist your learning. If you wish to take the vows to keep the precepts, I will ordain you as monks, nuns, upasakas, or upasikas, and will endeavor to live the Buddhist life with you. If you wish to donate material or immaterial thing, the monks will receive them in the name of the Dana-paramita. You need not worry how and where your seeds of charity are planted. Just give and forget. This is the way to maintain the Sangha, the group of practical Buddhists. No guest of the Buddhist house should worry about spreading the teaching or maintaining the movement. His time should be utilized in meditation, understanding the scriptures, and practicing what he is learning in his own world. This is the true spirit by which the teaching of Buddha will remain among mankind in its proper form.

Of course, I have no objection to your starting your own movement with the understanding you have attained, but while you are coming to this meditation hall, I wish you to be the "silent partner" of Zen. Throw out your ideas of teaching others, and devote yourselves to study—there are one thousand seven hundred kōans that you have to pass. There are five thousand books on Buddhism in European languages, which require your reading. And as for realization, once you think you have attained something, you will find yourself ten thousand feet below and have to start at the bottom again.

I am telling you this in such a severe way because I want you to attain the real, Buddhist enlightenment. There are many teachings from the Orient, but none of them can lead you to true enlightenment, true emancipation, except Zen Buddhism. They may satisfy your worldly desires, which they call spiritual attainment, but they will not lead you to the highest stage of Nirvana; you will drop to the world of dust again as an arrow shot toward the heavens falls to earth. What I say is the echo of my teacher's wisdom, and what my teacher told me is the wisdom of his teacher. We can trace directly through history seventy-nine generations of teachers to Buddha Sakyamuni. I shall tell you how to discipline yourselves until you are ready to practice Zen meditation. I could give you a longer discourse, but until you are ready to enter Samadhi, the more you hear about the theories and speculations, the more you will carry the unnecessary burden upon your shoulders.

I wish all of you to come practice the true Buddhism, following the discipline of Zen monks, and forgetting your own self-limited, worldly opinions.

September 19, 1933

Appendix: Cross-reference List of Chinese Names

I. Arranged alphabetically by Chinese readings

CHINESE	JAPANESE	CHARACTERS
Ch'an-yüeh	Zengetsu	禪月
Chang-ch'ing	Chōkei	長慶
Chang-shêng	Chōsei	長生
Chao-ch'ang	Jōshō	趙昌
Chao-chou	Jōshū	趙州
Chên-ts'ao	Chinsō	陳操
Chi-ch'ê	Keitetsu	繼徹
Chia-shan	Kassan	夾山
Ch'ien-fêng	Kembō	乾峰
Ch'ien-yüan	Zengen	漸源
Ch'in-shan	Kinzan	欽山
Ching-ch'ing	Kyōsei	鏡清
Chung-kuo-shih	Chūgokushi	忠國師
Chung-t'a	Chūdatsu	仲達
Chu-yü	Shuyu	茱萸
Fa-yen	Hōgen	法眼
Fei-t'ien	Hiden	肥田
Fên-yang	Funyō	汾陽
Han-shan	Kanzan	寒山
Han-t'ui-chih	Kantaishi	韓退之
Hsiang-yen	Kyōgen	香嚴
Hsin-hsin-ming	Shinjinmei	信心銘
Hsing-hua	Kōke	興化
Hsiu-ching	Kyūjō	休靜
Hsüan-chüeh	Genkaku	玄覚
Hsüan-sha	Gensha	玄沙
Hsüeh-fêng	Seppō	雪峰
Hsüeh-tou	Setchō	雪竇
Hua-yen	Kegon	華嚴
Huan-chung	Kanchū	寰中
Huang-po	Ōbaku	黃檗
Huang-lung	Ōryū	黃龍
Hui-chung	Echū	慧忠
Hui-t'ang	Kaidō	晦堂
Hung-chih	Wanshi	宏智
I-chung	Gichū	義忠
Kao-t'ing	Kōtei	高亭
Kuan-ch'i	Kankei	灌溪
Kuang	Kō	光
Kuei-shan	Isan	潙山
K'ung-fu-tzu	Kōfushi	孔夫子
K'ung-ming	Kōmei	孔明
K'uo	Kaku	廓
K'uo-an	Kakuan	廓庵
Lao-tzu	Rōshi	老子
Lê-p'u	Rakufu	樂普
Li-hsi	Rishō	利蹤
Lin-chi	Rinzai	臨濟
Liu-kêng	Rikukō	陸亘

Lo-shan	Razan	羅山	Ta-yü	Daigu	大愚
Lu-tsu	Roso	魯祖	T'ai-tsung	Taishū	太宗
Lung-ya	Ryūge	龍牙	Tan-hsia	Tanka	丹霞
Ma-ku	Mayoku	麻谷	Tan-yüan	Tangen	耽源
Ma-tsu	Baso	馬祖	Tao-t'ung	Dōtsū	道通
Min-wang	Bin'ō	閩王	Tao-wu	Dōgo	道吾
Mu-chou	Bokushū	睦州	Tê-shan	Tokusan	徳山
Nan-ch'üan	Nansen	南泉	Ti-ts'ang	Jizō	地藏
Nan-yüeh	Nangaku	南岳	T'ien-tan	Dentan	田單
Pa-chiao	Bashō	芭蕉	T'ien-t'ung	Tendō	天童
Pa-ling	Haryō	巴陵	T'ou-tzu	Tōji	投子
Pai-chang	Hyakujō	百丈	Ts'ao-shan	Sōzan	曹山
Pai-ling	Hyakurei	百靈	Ts'ung-yung-lu	Shōyōroku	從容錄
Pai-yün	Hakuun	白雲	Ts'ui-yen	Suigan	翠巖
P'ang-yün	Hōun	龐蘊	Tung-shan	Tōzan	洞山
Pao-fu	Hofuku	保福	Tzu-hu	Shiko	子湖
Pao-shou	Hoju	保壽	T'zu-ming	Jimyō	慈明
Pi-yen-chi	Hekiganshū	碧巖集	Wu-tsu	Goso	五祖
San-shêng	Sanshō	三聖	Wu-yeh	Mugō	無業
San-t'ung-ch'i	Sandōkai	參同契	Yang-shan	Gyōzan	仰山
Shao-shan	Shōzan	韶山	Yen-t'ou	Gentō	巖頭
Shih-shuang	Sekisō	石霜	Ying-chên	Ōshin	應眞
Shih-t'ou	Sekitō	石頭	Yüan-wu	Engo	圜悟
Ssu-ma T'ou-t'o	Shiba Zuda	司馬頭陀	Yüeh-shan	Yakusan	藥山
Ta-hui	Daie	大恵	Yün-chü	Unko	雲居
Ta-kuei-shan	Daiisan	大潙山	Yün-fêng	Umpō	雲峰
Ta-sui	Daizui	大隋	Yün-mên	Ummon	雲門
Ta-t'a	Daidachi	大達	Yün-yen	Ungan	雲巖
Ta-tien	Daiten	大顛	Yü-ti	Uteki	迂頓
Ta-t'zu	Daiji	大慈			

II. *Arranged alphabetically by Japanese readings*

JAPANESE	CHINESE	CHARACTERS			
Bashō	Pa-chiao	芭蕉	Chinsō	Chên-ts'ao	陳操
Baso	Ma-tsu	馬祖	Chōkei	Chang-ch'ing	長慶
Bin'ō	Min-wang	閩王	Chōsei	Chang-shêng	長生
Bokushū	Mu-chou	睦州	Chūdatsu	Chung-t'a	仲達
			Chūkokushi	Chung-kuo-shih	忠國師

Daidachi	Ta-t'a	大達		Kankei	Kuan-ch'i	灌溪
Daie	Ta-hui	大恵		Kantaishi	Han-t'ui-chih	韓退之
Daigu	Ta-yü	大愚		Kanzan	Han-shan	寒山
Daiisan	Ta-kuei-shan	大潙山		Kassan	Chia-shan	夾山
Daiji	Ta-t'zu	大慈		Kegon	Hua-yen	華嚴
Daiten	Ta-tien	大顛		Keitetsu	Chi-ch'ê	繼徹
Daizui	Ta-sui	大隋		Kembō	Ch'ien-fêng	乾峰
Dentan	T'ien-tan	田單		Kinzan	Ch'in-shan	欽山
Dōgo	Tao-wu	道吾		Kō	Kuang	光
Dōtsū	Tao-t'ung	道通		Kōfushi	Kung-fu-tzu	孔夫子
Echū	Hui-chung	慧忠		Kōke	Hsing-hua	興化
Engo	Yüan-wu	圓悟		Kōmei	K'ung-ming	孔明
Funyō	Fên-yang	汾陽		Kōtei	Kao-t'ing	高亭
Gantō	Yen-t'ou	巖頭		Kyōgen	Hsiang-yen	香巖
Genkaku	Hsüan-chüeh	玄覺		Kyōsei	Ching-ch'ing	鏡清
Gensha	Hsüan-sha	玄沙		Kyūjō	Hsiu-ching	休靜
Gichū	I-chung	義忠		Mayoku	Ma-ku	麻谷
Goso	Wu-tsu	五祖		Mugō	Wu-yeh	無業
Gyōzan	Yang-shan	仰山		Nangaku	Nan-yüeh	南岳
Hakuun	Pai-yün	白雲		Nansen	Nan-ch'üan	南泉
Haryō	Pa-ling	巴陵		Ōbaku	Huang-po	黃檗
Hekiganshū	Pi-yen-chi	碧巖集		Ōryū	Huang-lung	黃龍
Hiden	Fei-t'ien	肥田		Ōshin	Ying-chên	應眞
Hofuku	Pao-fu	保福		Rakufu	Lê-p'u	樂普
Hōgen	Fa-yen	法眼		Razan	Lo-shan	羅山
Hoju	Pao-shou	保壽		Rikukō	Liu-kêng	陸亙
Hōun	P'ang-yün	龐蘊		Rinzai	Lin-chi	臨濟
Hyakujō	Pai-chang	百丈		Rishō	Li-hsi	利蹤
Hyakurei	Pai-ling	百靈		Rōshi	Lao-tzu	老子
Isan	Kuei-shan	潙山		Roso	Lu-tsu	魯祖
Jimyō	T'zu-ming	慈明		Ryūge	Lung-ya	龍牙
Jizō	Ti-ts'ang	地藏		Sandōkai	San-t'ung-ch'i	參同契
Jōshō	Chao-ch'ang	趙昌		Sanshō	San-shêng	三聖
Jōshū	Chao-chou	趙州		Sekisō	Shih-shuang	石霜
Kaidō	Hui-t'ang	晦堂		Sekitō	Shih-t'ou	石頭
Kaku	K'uo	廓		Seppō	Hsüeh-fêng	雪峰
Kakuan	K'uo-an	廓庵		Setchō	Hsüeh-tou	雪竇
Kanchū	Huan-chung	寰中		Shiba Zuda	Ssu-ma T'ou-t'o	司馬頭陀

Shinjinmei	Hsin-hsin-ming	信心銘
Shiko	Tzu-hu	子湖
Shōyōroku	Ts'ung-yung-lu	從容錄
Shōzan	Shao-shan	韶山
Shuyu	Chu-yü	茱萸
Sōzan	Ts'ao-shan	曹山
Suigan	Ts'ui-yen	翠巖
Taishū	T'ai-tsung	太宗
Tangen	Tan-yüan	耽源
Tanka	Tan-hsia	丹霞
Tendō	T'ien-t'ung	天童
Tōji	T'ou-tzu	投子

Tokusan	Tê-shan	德山
Tōzan	Tung-shan	洞山
Ummon	Yün-mên	雲門
Umpō	Yün-fêng	雲峰
Ungan	Yün-yen	雲巖
Unko	Yün-chü	雲居
Uteki	Yü-ti	迂頔
Wanshi	Hung-chih	宏智
Yakusan	Yüeh-shan	藥山
Zengen	Ch'ien-yüan	漸源
Zengetsu	Ch'an-yüeh	禪月

Glossary

Asterisks indicate terms that are explained elsewhere in the glossary. The abbreviations J. and C. stand respectively for "Japanese" and "Chinese."

Analects, The: an account of the manners and sayings of Confucius, composed of material gathered daily by his disciples.

Avalokiteçvara (*J.* Kannon, *C.* Kwan-yin): a lay disciple of early Buddhism, later known as the Bodhisattva of Compassion.

Bodhi: enlightened wisdom in its highest sense. It is the source of Prajna* and Karuna.*

Bodhidharma (*J.* Daruma, *C.* Ta-ma): known also as the "Blue-eyed Monk "; he is credited with first bringing Zen from India to China in the sixth century.

Bodhisattva: a person dedicated not only to his own enlightenment but also to the enlightenment of all sentient beings.

Buddha: enlightend one. May refer to Gautama Buddha or to any enlightened person.

Buddha-Dharma: enlightened wisdom.

Çravaka: one who seeks to purify himself of greed, anger, and ignorance, but who has not yet experienced enlightenment.

Dharma: the content of enlightenment to be realized intuitively, directly, and personally experienced.

Dharmakaya: the law body of the Buddha, the eternal Buddha.

Diamond Sutra: the full title in Sanscrit is Vajracchedika-prajna-paramita-sutra, but is more commonly known as the Vajracchedika, or by its English name, or by its Japanese name, the Kongō-kyō.

Five Precepts: these are the fundamental precepts to be followed by all Buddhists: not to take life, not to steal, not to indulge in sensuality, not to lie, and not to become intoxicated by drink or drugs.

Four Vows: to save all sentient beings, to destroy all evil passions, to learn all sacred teachings, to follow the path of Buddhahood despite all difficulties.

Hinayana: one of the two main branches of Buddhism; *see* Mahayana.

Karma: the law of cause and effect. A noun coming from the verb *kar,* meaning "to do." All states and conditions in life are the direct results of previous actions, and each action in the present determines the fate of the future. Life is the working process of Karma, the endless sequence of cause and effect.

Karuna: compassion.

Kōan (*C.* kung-an): a problem given to a student by a teacher. It cannot be solved by intellection, but must be answered from the student's own experience. Some monasteries use it today as part of their displayed ritual, but this practice is frowned upon by those who have achieved enlightenment.

Mahayana: commonly translated as "Greater Vehicle" as opposed to Hinayana, or "Lesser Vehicle." These are the two great divisions of Buddhist teaching. Hinayana teaches the enlightenment of the individual and uses the Pali texts.* Mahayana stresses the need of enlightenment as a means of enlightening all sentient beings and uses other texts in addition to the Tripitaka.* Both branches, however, are united in the precepts as well as in other major phases of the teaching and are very tolerant of one another.

Maitreya (*J.* Miroku, *C.* Mi-leh): the Buddha yet to appear in the world.

Manjusri (*J.* Monju, *C.* Wen-sha): a Bodhisattva, often depicted riding a lion, holding a sword and a book. Considered to be the personification of wisdom.

Nirvana: synonymous with enlightenment. It is not the negative condition of nothingness or non-existance, as translated by many scholars.

Pali texts: the Pitakas were first committed to writing in Pali, one of the early languages of Buddhism. They are the texts used especially in the Hinayana school.

Paramita: the six virtues of Buddhism: Dana, charity; Sila, morality; Kshanti, patience; Virya, perseverence; Dhyana, meditation; Prajna, intuitive wisdom.

Parinirvana: beyond the nirvana which can be experienced in life.

Patriarchs: Bodhidharma is considered the first of the Chinese patriarchs of which there were five.

Prajna: wisdom.

Samadhi: that condition achieved by the practice of meditation.

Samantabhadra (*J.* Fugen, *C.* P'u-hsien): Bodhisattva of Love, usually depicted riding an elephant. Manjusri (wisdom) and Samantabhadra (love) are the two aspects of Buddha (enlightenment).

Samsara: the world of birth and death.

Sangha: the monastic order founded by Buddha. In Mahayana it also includes any group of laymen dedicated to the Dharma.

Sanzen: the examination of a student by a teacher. This may take place at any time over any incident which may prompt it, but, in general, the student goes to the master's room alone for the examination. This usually takes place twice a day except during Sesshin,* when a master may receive a student four or five times in the course of a day to see what progress he is making with his kōan.

Sarira: gems supposed to be found in the ashes of Buddhist saints after cremation.

Satori (*C.* wu): enlightenment.

Sesshin: a special period of intensified meditation. One week of each month is usually set aside for sesshin. Only the most essential work of the monastery is done during this period.

Shastra: also Sastra. Commentary on the sutras.

Subhuti: one of the Çravakas.*

Sufi: member of a sect of Islam developed in Persia.

Sutra: collective name for Buddhist scriptures.

Tathagata: variously translated as Buddha, Mind Essence, Eternal Presence, Eternal Now.

Tripitaka: literally, "three baskets." Used to refer to the entire body of Buddhist scriptures.

Upasaka: a lay disciple who strives to keep the Five Precepts* at all times.

Upasika: feminine form of Upasaka.

Zazen: to sit in Zen meditation.

Zen-dō: the room used for Zen meditation or, in a monastery, the meditation hall.

Bibliography

Herrigel, Eugen: *Zen in the Art of Archery,* Pantheon Books Inc., New York, 1953

Leggett, Trevor: *A First Zen Reader,* Charles E. Tuttle Company, Rutland & Tokyo, 1960

Reps, Paul: *Zen Flesh, Zen Bones,* Charles E. Tuttle Company, Rutland & Tokyo, 1957

Senzaki, Nyogen, and Ruth S. McCandless: *Buddhism and Zen,* Philosophical Library Inc., New York, 1953

Suzuki, Dr. Daisetz Teitaro: *Essays in Zen Buddhism: First Series,* Rider & Co., London, 1949

———: *Essays in Zen Buddhism: Second Series,* Rider & Co., London, 1950

———: *Essays in Zen Buddhism: Third Series,* Rider & Co., London, 1953

———: *The Zen Doctrine of No-Mind,* Rider & Co., London, 1949

———: *Zen and Japanese Buddhism,* Japan Travel Bureau, Tokyo, 1958